CW00736105

© 2024 by Niels de Fraguier
www.cartographyofinnerworlds.com

Cover illustration by Henry Rivers

Book illustrations by Niels de Fraguier

First edition, November 2024
ISBN 979-10-415-5821-6

No part of this publication may be reproduced, distributed, or
transmitted in any form or by any means, including photocopying,
recording, or other electronic or mechanical methods, without the
prior written permission of the author, except in the case of brief
quotations embodied in critical reviews and certain other
noncommercial uses permitted by copyright law.

CARTOGRAPHY OF INNER WORLDS

A Journey to Deepen the Meaning of Our Lives

Niels de Fraguier

This exploration does not pretend to provide solutions but opens up questions to inquire about the change you want to find within yourself to live a meaningful life. It aims to expand your thinking and feeling so that you can lead positive change in your life and the world. It was written by a privileged white straight male born and raised in the Global North.

CONTENTS

To all fellow human beings of the Earth and the ones to come.

'WE[1] ARE THE ONES'

From 'being', we have been compelled to 'having', cradled in the illusion of consumption, acceleration, and competition being the main factors of a so-called 'successful life'. Pulled in many directions, we lose our ability to focus on what makes our lives meaningful. This distraction disconnects us from being at peace with ourselves, others and the living world.

But on the eve of a necessary world metamorphosis, driven by mounting social and ecological pressures, we have the unique opportunity to reinvent our way of being in the world.

What if there was another path? A path that enables us to live true to ourselves and in service to future generations. A path in which we use our attention, love, and energy wisely for what really matters. A path that empowers us to become the pioneers of our lives.

---

[1] *The word 'we' is used throughout the book. The choice to use this term comes with great respect and appreciation for everyone's unique identity while encompassing the need to join forces to build a collective wave of change. 'We' is enriched by the many realities and situations of individuals all having diverse needs and aspirations.*

Cartography of Inner Worlds invites you to explore a radically new story. By opening a breach to plant new seeds, the book takes you on an exploratory and transformational journey towards your future self and a future worth our children's children. It supports you to initiate a journey of self-discovery to create a more meaningful life for yourself and contribute to a flourishing future.

This is the journey I began at the age of 19 when I left the place I used to call 'home'. Shaped by the tumultuous separation of my parents as a young teenager, I ignored for years this childhood trauma that led me to adopt a parental role supporting my two younger brothers. This experience has taught me that transforming our lives begins with understanding and healing our past, living fully in the present, and actively shaping our future.

Living through what I could bring to them, I was disconnected from myself, others, and the world. When I saw them taking their paths, I felt the need for a breakthrough that could make me feel alive. I had enough of saying that I was alright; I was sick inside out. This led me to make the most rewarding decision of my life: looking after myself to serve others.

I would like to share with you that I came to this understanding because of the support I received in troubled times. Nevertheless, the feeling of lacking love, assistance and care led me to understand the value of giving others the support they deserve in their lives.

Thus, this book aims to empower you to inquire about yourself, dream about the future, and deliver on your aspirations. You will be immersed in content resulting from years of introspection, conversations with hundreds of people around the world who have shared their stories and struggles, and dozens of cultures that have taught me how diversity can enrich our lives.

Cartography of Inner Worlds is a gentle invitation for you to join a practical and hopeful journey of shaping yourself to contribute to a better world. From exploring your identity to questioning your perception of the world, you will be invited on an empowering journey of self-discovery to unveil yourself to life.

Through real-life stories, accessible ideas, and practical inquiries, the book will take you on an exciting adventure demonstrating that another way is not only desirable but possible.

Inspired by the Japanese word 'Komorebi', Cartography of Inner Worlds will empower you to see the light in yourself and the world to live meaningfully. Together, we embark on an adventure that will enable you to thrive on a meaningful journey on Earth—for you to feel your heartbeat, your body tingle and your eyes spark again.

INTRODUCTION

From political instability to climate change, our generation is facing what could be the most significant threats humanity has ever faced. Our systems are getting closer to points of non-return where irreparable damage already creates suffering, trauma, and loss for many. At the core of this gigantic machine are the pilots: us. We are part of the eight billion citizens on this planet, fuelling the system every day through every choice we make, actions we take, and ideals we support. Often despite our will, we are the victims and perpetrators of the harm we witness. Imprisoned by the invisible cage of the system, we are missing out on the influence of the structures shaping every single step we make in life. We are enslaved by the obsolete processor running our societies as part of a system operating from the past, taking us to an unstable present and leading us to a perilous future.

In an ever-growing addiction to growth, acceleration and domination, I am worried that we have missed the point of what life should be about. We have forgotten about our true selves—becoming the reflection of expectations lying over our heads and being taken away from who we are. The world order has taken citizens down, making us invisible and shutting down our originality.

We became unseen by moulding ourselves into pursuing the growth imperative, cradled by the sick pace of the world. This societal machinery projects the necessity to rush after status, wealth, and titles.

Losing sense of who we are, we support the madness of the old paradigm against our will. We are squeezed and pushed to the extreme to favour productivity using resources as though they are unlimited. While humans make up just 0.01% of all living beings[2], we have already left a significant footprint on other life forms. Our species has overtaken natural resources to grow economically. From massive deforestation to increased CO_2 emissions and land domestication, we have grown our economy and ideals with financial profit as the only indicator of value creation. Society's pursuit of expansion has resulted in rising temperatures, massive biodiversity loss, water scarcity, and many other impacts harmful to life. In following this path, we have torn apart many of the natural ecosystems that are essential to safeguarding life on Earth, prioritising growth at all costs against nature and human dignity.

The state of our planet is crystal clear: we are hitting new average temperature records every recent year, forcing an increasing number of individuals to flee their homes, while we witness an average 69% drop in mammals, birds,

---

[2] *Humans represent just 0.01% of all life but have destroyed 83% of wild mammals, The Guardian.*

fish, reptiles, and amphibian populations since 1970[3]. We cannot turn a blind eye to the catastrophe we are heading for if nothing changes. We are at war with the conditions enabling us to live on Earth.

The breadth of the issue is enormous, and we are on the course for unprecedented tipping points. Reaching these could deregulate the balance of adequate conditions for life on Earth. The temperature rise we already witness leads to catastrophic changes in our lives with floods, wildfires, and heatwaves impacting food production, human migration, health, and living conditions across all continents. That could just be the beginning.

All these anthropic changes come from our dominant mindset on a planet where resources are limited and can regenerate only if cared for. Disconnected from the living world, we have forgotten our intrinsic connection to nature running after the expansion dream of infinite progress. But progress for what and for whom? In always going for more and with higher speed, we face our own limits.

Driven by the obsolete story of domination, we run the world frantically keeping ourselves occupied with meaningless tasks while the old system dictates society's evolution. The pace of our existence leaves little space for questioning our actual lives. When the value is focused on economic production, there is no room for self-exploration of identity, emotions and aspirations. In looking away from

---

[3] *WWF Living Planet Report: Devastating 69% drop in wildlife populations since 1970, October 2022.*

the essentials, we are distracted by constant noise. This noise of meaningless events drives us away from taking time to know and love ourselves. When one thinks about their place on this planet, they are biased to think through the eyes of the system. Our reference becomes what the world has projected onto us.

This formatting encourages us to experience and feel scarcity—not having enough. We are set up to want, own, and control more and more. This obsession makes our personalities and unique talents melt into the masses. All wanting the same, we compete against each other when we could put our forces together. We slowly disappear to become nullified, losing our vast potential for thriving.

Rushing into what we can still get makes us unable to slow down and appreciate what surrounds us. On the verge of falling apart individually, we grasp the last branches of existence to survive. We do our best in the worst conditions without giving it a real chance to live fully. We are pushed towards the edge and convince ourselves that following the herd is the safest thing to do. All this results in supporting the establishment and, therefore, the status quo, taking away meaning from our lives. Most of us fade away into what is expected of us rather than expanding to who we truly desire to become. Moved away from our thriving, we are collectively pressured to stay aboard the train heading to catastrophe.

But if humanity has lost its way now, this doesn't mean the story is over. On the contrary, it is time for enlightenment, where we can help one another write a new story. We are given the unique opportunity to unleash a tale that sheds light on the beauty of human nature, where self-awareness, curiosity, and collaboration can become the new parameters of a desirable future. This story should no longer be about following the existing but rather creating the new in service to who we are and want to become.

Humanity's future is on hold and our awakening is the way forward for a thriving future. As the artists of our lives, we are the creators of what is yet to come. Assuming our role of custodians, we hold the keys. The time has come to be—reconnecting with self, others, and the world.

Cartography of Inner Worlds invites you to seize the lifetime you have ahead to make it a meaningful experience. This time on Earth is worth the adventure of encounters, experiences, and emotions. While your existence and perception of the world may sometimes feel like a dark journey, we are about to explore how to find the light that can help us move from the linearity of our existence to feel alive again.

This book is a source of hope. Let's explore what the present and future could look like through the lens of possibilities.

PART 1

SELF-INTROSPECTION

As we initiate this journey together, let's ensure you look after yourself while approaching this self-introspection. Trust your intuition and feelings to make this exploration a meaningful adventure. There is no right or wrong emotion, feeling, or question. All are legitimate, and you should welcome them as they come.

You might have questions, and you do not need to seek instant answers. Instead, do not hesitate to write down what comes to your mind, accepting to inquire about your feelings. This part of the book might trigger some emotions and reveal hidden parts of yourself. Take the time you need and deserve to reflect on the various inquiries, leaving space for the unknown.

Accepting that you don't have all the answers will be a major step in this experience. Every insight you feel will bring you closer to the most adequate pathway that fits your needs and the future you want to carve for yourself. Let's deep dive together with a gentle attitude towards ourselves.

CHAPTER ONE

WHERE DO YOU COME FROM?

—

'We may not be responsible for the world that created our minds, but we can take responsibility for the mind with which we create our world.'

Gabor Mate

I have been in transhumance for many years, exploring diverse places and communities around the globe. On my diverse travels, one recurring question was always at the start of new encounters: 'Where do you come from?'. I always related to the notion of geographical space, but with time, I realised that people define their origin on various levels: city, community, country, or ethnicity. I had the chance to reflect on this usual question to give it depth and meaning. What if our origins were beyond a geographical location? I realised that I was coming from a place of trauma with the legacy of the tumultuous divorce of my parents at the age of twelve. Left with the feeling of being betrayed and abandoned, my little world collapsed with what appeared to me at this time extremely violent. The situation led me to adopt a parental role to protect my younger siblings from the turmoil already taking me to the next chapter of my life.

Without realising it, I missed many of the stages a teenager can get to experience, abruptly transitioning to adulthood. The trauma was so profound that all of my childhood memories have since been erased, leaving me as an adult with a blank canvas. Shutting myself down to avoid feeling and accepting the pain, I built myself upon an unstable foundation that started eroding with time, letting cracks appear.

This traumatic start of my existence was unveiled in all my life experiences, calling me to make an effort to understand, acknowledge and heal. My first reaction was, therefore, to look for novelty, leaving the place I used to call 'home' to explore myself through new experiences with diverse cultures, people, and realities. I had this invisible and unconscious inner fire calling on me to be bold. To quit what I always knew as the unknown was the ultimate opportunity to finally start living according to who I was. It felt like a life bet jumping into the future.

Taking this decision helped me to reach the place where I needed to be and start a more profound personal work. From ignoring the scars of my early life journey, I made the scary step of focusing and reflecting on what shaped my existence, using these painful events as enablers to heal and finally live according to what was to become. I did not accept being stuck anymore in the past. This decision set me on track to healing, carving a path towards a more peaceful existence. It also enabled me to heal the traumas I was carrying while reflecting on the importance of reducing the likelihood of perpetuating them for future generations.

This experience invited me to make a connection to the story of human beings. Over 13.8 billion years of cosmic history, the emergence of human beings was a mere blip, taking place just 300,000 years ago. Despite our relatively short existence, accounting for only 0.002% of the time since the Big Bang, the last century has seen the unravelling harm caused by humans on the planet—demonstrating our immaturity as a species. This civilisational legacy has led us to be who we are today. Generations have transitioned from community-driven to individualistic approaches in recent years, influenced by the capitalist lens of societies. The primacy of the individual has taken over as a rule, influencing our lives. Detaching slowly from this sense of community, we have progressively lost our attachment to others and place.

As this evolution shaped who we are today, returning to our origins and understanding where our society has developed seems essential. This can help us be in harmony with the birthing of our personalities to build a thriving existence, being part of life through our common origins and diverse personal stories. Let's remind ourselves that we are all citizens of one place called the pale blue dot. Earth. The planet is hosting us on its land that we, human beings, share as our home.

EXPLORING YOUR ROOTS

Being aware of where we come from is the way to start. Our existences have multiple facets that make us who we are today. We have inherited the sum of events, fears, and traumas that are still part of our DNA[4] today. For generations, we have passed on these fears that unconsciously affect our daily behaviours and decisions. These fears can be classified under three main categories: lack, confrontation, and exclusion.

The fear of lacking comes from previous crises that have happened throughout time, with food or money shortages leading to hunger and poverty. We have been conditioned to save what we have so we do not miss out on the future. The fear of confrontation results from our hunter-gatherer spirit, which has made us defend ourselves from predators and rivals—such as other individuals seen as more powerful or illnesses jeopardising survival. This animosity against others comes from the fright of facing dangers that could threaten our survival. The third is the fear of exclusion from communities and groups, which separates us from the social life we need to develop our personalities. We are tweaked to defend our status acquired through social connections and, therefore, will do everything not to be excluded from groups.

From these fears, we have developed the drive to accumulate in order not to lack, dominate not be threatened, and conform not to be separated from the crowd. These fears are elements that are part of our

---

[4] *The DNA (deoxyribonucleic acid) is a molecule that contains the genetic instructions used in the development and functioning of all known living organisms.*

identities today. Until we initiate the work to acknowledge, reflect, and heal them, we will keep perpetrating something that has been going on for many generations. This is what we inherited from previous generations who have shaped the place we live in, our beliefs, and the land we live on. From the culture of our country, the education of our close ones, the history of the land, to the beliefs of our life mentors, we have initiated this life journey with significant influences. Our stories have started on a prewritten book, sourcing its inspiration from previous generations.

Understanding how the story has been inspired and what events have shaped its meaning is where our energy needs to be invested. We are called to acknowledge that our existences depart from before our arrival on the Earth and will last way beyond our lifetime. We are passengers of the Earth with a heritage that will last for centuries.

Imagine yourself being a tree surrounded by others, making us a gigantic forest. Trees take their foundations into the soil. Using their roots to source nutrients and energy, their strengths and flexibility directly come from their link to the ground. In need of great soil to grow and expand, they get affected by the quality of it, such as we do with our past—inheriting from previous genes and history. Their deep connection to the soil grows with time, giving the tree more strength to source energy and resist weather events. They become more resilient to change and increase their capacity to resist, adapt, and thrive. This is precisely what happens to us with life events, giving us more depth and strength with years of life rooted in the soil of centuries.

We arrived on this Earth as a seed planted into the fertile ground of past generations—inheriting from traumas, wisdom, and culture of the past. Too little to be living on our own, we have relied on others to survive. With time and care for the most fortunate, we have evolved into a shrub, growing our roots and building branches to gain independence. Over time, we keep lengthening roots and branches, expanding ourselves—sourcing energy from the soil we have grown up in. The soil is the fertile ground for thriving as well as suffering. It gathers all our ancestors' experiences, significantly influencing our path in life. We have to get to know our roots to understand our past, live in the present, and co-create a thriving future healing with our ancestral traumas.

HEALING OUR CULTURE OF TRAUMA

As we entered the world, we took on our shoulders the history of many before us. We inherited the weight of our cultural, environmental, social, and economic heritage. The unresolved scars of previous generations have been left for us to deal with. Many of us have inherited and lived harmful situations such as trauma, neglect and abuse. To better understand its meaning, let's look at the origin of the word trauma, which means wound in Greek. It is a scar cured only in appearance but that remains unhealed deep inside. Trauma is like a broken bone covered by healthy skin. It remains hidden under what seems to be fine but is unresolved inside. It harms our whole equilibrium. When a life event has traumatised individuals, and they have not done the work to heal it, the likelihood of this trauma being transmitted to future generations is high. While we all have experienced traumas, they have very diverse levels of importance and incidence in our lives.

Each of us has its own history living within our mind, body, and soul. Trauma is there without us being able to feel it and, most of the time, make sense of it. While immaterial and often unconscious, the pain of past suffering is deep inside us. Our defence mechanism makes us bury the pain deep inside so that it does not appear in our conscious day-to-day. Nevertheless, it influences our unconscious and, therefore, our decisions, emotions, and relationships. Our natural response is to run away from pain and ignore traumas, anaesthetising ourselves from the problem.

The fear of facing the difficult moments of our lives goes hand in hand with the frenetic pace of our existence, making our escape from the core. Running away only leads to more pain in the long term, with unresolved internal conflicts stopping us from being free. We hope to be stable without proper foundations on which we can stand. Imagine building a weak house in a seismic area. An earthquake would ruin it instantly.

The weight of our scars is following us like a shadow that will never leave us until we acknowledge and heal it. Think of your shadow as an obscure shape stretching out behind you. It is the collection of all your life events that have added weight to your existence, with unresolved struggles adding to each other. Imagine yourself pulling an invisible weight for every single movement you make. It does not simply represent a mental burden but also influences how you build relationships, behave, trust, belong, relate, imagine, feel, perceive or love.

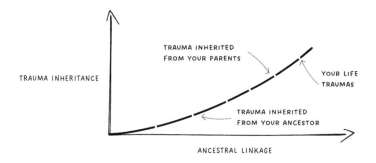

Figure 1: Throughout generations, we inherit traumas becoming our shadow part. Until we sit with them, they will keep on being perpetrated to future generations.

These unresolved troubles can be the ones that influence individuals to become toxic leaders, putting society at risk with attitudes that are destructive towards the world at large. From politics to business, we see a growing trend of traumatised leaders in power. Their behaviours are often the results of a detachment from their feelings and emotions. Until we accept to look inside ourselves, we will continue repeating our misguided behaviours.

If we look at the world today, all the crises we face relate to our mental injuries. We have put our planet in trauma, jeopardising its natural balance. We have put local traditions in trauma by imposing the standards of the Western world. We have put indigenous people in trauma by taking away their culture. We have put our societies in trauma, losing the essential trust we need to enable democratic participation. We have put our brains in trauma with screens diminishing our cognitive abilities. The list goes on. The crisis is within us and not external to who we are. We are in trauma mode, driving ourselves crazy and putting others at risk with amplified contamination of traumas to spread if we do not heal the core.

For this reason, the fundamental work is to look at our shadow side to understand where we are truly coming from. This healing process takes shape by deconstructing the blocks that have been on our way and become hurdles to our flourishing. From the shadow part, we need to put these into the light. The burdens we have been dragging can become steps to the stairs we are building for a wiser and more meaningful life.

Awareness of such barriers is essential so we are not unconsciously biased when interacting with the world. Expanding from traumas enables us to transform burdens into energy, inform our future decisions, and help us live in the present moment. Traumas are positive drivers when healed as they inform us about future life experiences. They show us how to live fully in the present rather than being unconsciously burdened by the past.

LEVERAGING THE PAST

If trauma is contagious, healing can also be for the better. It can become a driving force for positive change in our world. We can inspire and help others heal from our healing, to live in harmony with our past, present, and future. Beyond our well-being, it is our duty not to perpetrate harm to future generations. As we evolve in a world characterised by the shame of feeling, you can ask yourself whether you want to live in peace with your true self, letting go of the pain and giving space to live fully.

The process can be challenging as strengths and power are often the most rewarded identity attributes. It can often be shameful and fearful for us to look inside ourselves and explore the dark hours of our lives. Ashamed to accept who we truly are, it seems easy to take the shortcut of ignorance. Nevertheless, it is crucial to do the work as our bodies keep the score[5] by memorising traumatic events.

When traumatised, we feel unsafe inside our bodies with an internal discomfort, making us detach from our gut feelings and hide behind a false identity. If previous experiences tweak our thinking, facing the truth and understanding how we perceive the world based on our past is crucial. To heal is to become at ease with the sensations of our body and mind. It is essential to acknowledge that we will always be within the body we have today. Despite its aesthetic and psychological changes with life experiences,

---

[5] *The Body Keeps the Score: Brain, Mind, and Body in the Healing of Trauma, Bessel van der Kolk M.D.*

your body will remain the house in which you will live during your lifespan. This place you inhabit will never host anyone else and is your space to feel, live, and grow in peace. Ensuring you tidy up your home is essential to attain clarity of thought and perception of what the world offers.

Consider every experience you lived as a springboard taking you further. For each event, there are takeaways to learn from and collect. Our lives are enriched by the number of events we live and their intensity. As part of natural systems, we have a powerful ability to bounce back in difficult times. We grow from every new situation, being compelled to find a way to keep moving forward with care and time. What is important is not to bounce back quickly but to recover correctly. We have climbed many summits in the past and will need to climb many other ones across the stages of our lives.

If our histories are heavily rooted in the past, grasping its comprehensive reality is essential to look into the future. It is a complex journey. Identifying traumas will not happen overnight, but having a solid intention to work on it is vital. To set the intention in itself is an accomplishment. It is the starting point of being open to healing and caring for ourselves. Doing this work is a way to liberate yourself from the alienation of the past. It is the opportunity to step up to a new chapter of your life where learning can drive your exploration towards exciting pathways of life. In the journey, many can help us to enrich your reflection. Everyone around you has a role to play, from those who have lived traumatic experiences to the ones who have perpetrated these events.

The real work of healing takes courage and vulnerability to inspire your inquiry. Be ready, as this will affect your entire existence. Now is the time to step up and lead with your heart, mind and soul to explore the deepest parts of yourself.

KEY TAKEAWAYS

1. We inherit the history of previous generations stored in our minds and bodies. It influences our way of being from a place of unconsciousness.

2. Traumas are part of us. Identifying them is essential to understanding our place in the world and shaping the future we want to create.

3. While invisible to us, we all carry a shadow part that follows us in daily life, influencing our decisions and impacting our existence. This shadow goes beyond a mental burden as it influences how you build relationships, behave, trust, belong, relate, imagine, feel, perceive, or love.

4. When we experience challenging situations, we are gifted with precious takeaways that can help us better understand who we are and the direction we want to take in life. They are a springboard to the next stage of our existence.

5. Healing ourselves is the way to live a more meaningful existence and avoid passing down our traumas to future generations.

PRACTICAL REFLECTIONS

→ What are the key events that have brought pain to your life?

→ How are you carrying these events as part of your shadow? How could you work on them so that you heal with your past?

→ When has your life changed trajectory to arrive where you are today?

→ What can you learn from the challenging times of your life?

→ What would it look like if you had to draw a line representing your existence?

→ How and what do you record from your childhood?

→ Draw a tree to examine where you source the person you are (roots), what makes you stable (trunk), what you are exploring (branches), and what you feel from each of these experiences (leaves).[6]

---

[6] *Find practical tools and self-introspection exercises, such as The Tree of Life, on the book's website: cartographyofinnerworlds.com*

CHAPTER TWO

WHO ARE YOU?

—

'Be yourself; everyone else is already taken.'
Oscar Wilde

I experienced first-hand the life we can live outside of ourselves. The pain of my early years and the fear of facing new traumas led me to erect walls around myself, cutting off my emotions and pretending I was okay. I was running away from myself, convinced that the problem would disappear on its own. I built a shield by putting all my energy and love towards my younger siblings—using the attention towards them as a wall to avoid looking after my own life. I convinced myself that being in service to them was the right thing to do: losing track of my path and living through them. This detachment from self took me away from my core by creating an alias that was not true to who I was. I filled the virtual 'me' with anything that could seem cheerful and happy, building a facade for my authentic self. I wanted to be in control of the uncertainty that scared me off with a dominant attitude towards my feelings, pushing them away and denying their intensity.

The denial of my vulnerability cut me off from the world and myself, pretending to be okay while the sadness was growing. It slowly isolated me from the world, disengaging with others out of fear of showing some weaknesses and being triggered with deeper scars. It took me away from welcoming emotions and enjoying the present moment. I was passively living, building another 'I' for people around me not to ask how I felt and for me not to work on who I was.

My early life situation informed my travels as I encountered people defining themselves differently. I met many of them building fake identities to avoid facing their deepest scars, as well as others fully welcoming their quest for identity. Inspired by all these encounters, I understood that I needed to deconstruct this second self to refocus on being the only person I was. The time had come for me to welcome my identity with all its imperfections, emotions, and blisters to live in abundance with myself, adopting a multi-layer perspective.

It was then that I realised the importance of analysing our beliefs about who we are. From our gender to our political opinions, we see ourselves through our own perspective. Our identities are multiple and can evolve. We are a unit interacting with the world around us, including other people, communities, institutions, and history. Knowing who we are is about understanding what brought us to our position at this particular moment in time. It can help us better understand how to live in harmony with ourselves, others, and the world.

Most of us grew up in a world where rewarding status and wealth are the leading indicators of success. Work is often presented as the primary determinant of our identities. The imperative of being productive calls us to create economic value. What we own and produce is a way to tell ourselves and others who we are. This is diverting us from the essential piece: self-esteem.

The system has developed pathological traits driven by competition, moving us far from our core. It has ranked individuals too often based on their financial success. We live in fears and desires, believing that 'having' equates to 'being'. Projected into us, we tend to define ourselves with things we own, the work positions we hold, or even the social connections we have. The current paradigm tells you that the higher you stand on the 'hierarchy of society', the better you should feel about yourself—leaving us too often unsatisfied. We always aim for the next thing to have. We fill our 'emptiness' with stuff to forget about the actual work we need to do on ourselves.

From the simplicity of being authentic, we have been encouraged to become consumers[7] who believe in the society-crafted story, being offered many options to pursue our self-interest. This makes us think that we take control of our lives, becoming the master of our destiny through the choices we are invited to make. It makes us forget that our options are only part of a limited list imposed by the

---

[7] *Citizens: Why the Key to Fixing Everything is All of Us, Jon Alexander.*

establishment. It is like choosing your dish from a menu without having the option to make your own recipe.

As we shape ourselves into what is expected, we want to be seen and valued by others. We support the system principles under which owning things, creating monetary value, and taking control is called success. Craving for status, we too often run from our true identities. We make a story that fits the mainstream narrative, renouncing to unveil our real identity. The time has come for us to reclaim our identities: welcoming our unique traits and personality.

RECOGNISING OUR IDENTITIES AND PRIVILEGES

As introduced previously, we have all been shaped by events that have made us who we are today. We have designed our identities for each of these lived experiences. We are asked to tick the boxes of a world that has gone mainstream. For many years, we have been told that we could only be either a woman or a man, single or in a relationship, rich or poor, educated or not. Even if this tends to evolve with the recognition of multiple identities, standardising ourselves impoverishes our contribution to the world and creates shame for those outside the mainstream. Judged for being different, anyone going off track risks the reprisal of the crowd—being excluded or stereotyped. The social construct phenomenon shuts down creativity and weakens the richness of social interactions.

Reclaiming our identities is essential to feeling alive. It can enable us to express our whole selves with our entire identity through all its forms and unleash our unique contribution to the world. When we define ourselves dualistically, we forget that we have multiple traits. We do not have to be either or.

Our real asset is to leverage the diversity of our lived experiences and the wealth of multiculturalism around us to stand for who we truly are. To do so, we need to start by understanding our identities and their influence on the role we have been given in society. The concept of intersectionality[8] sums it up into an inspiring lens coined by Professor Kimberlé Crenshaw. The term defines the richness of our identities, acknowledging the complex relationship between social identities and systems of power and oppression. Our social identities intersect with one another and define our personalities about the world we live in. Multiple factors influence the person we are, evolving and transforming as we live.

Shaped by norms and beliefs, we are invited to reflect on our position to grasp the complete picture of who we are. Privileges are a crucial notion to explore when working on your self-introspection. They are special rights or advantages given to a particular individual or group. Privileges have always been part of our lives—whether we benefit from them or are adversely affected by others having them. For centuries, privileges have been transmitted from one generation to the next. For instance, if you are reading this book, you might already be part of the privileged group

---

[8] *On Intersectionality: Essential Writings, Kimberlé Crenshaw.*

with access to education. This opportunity might be the result of your parents and ancestors' education.

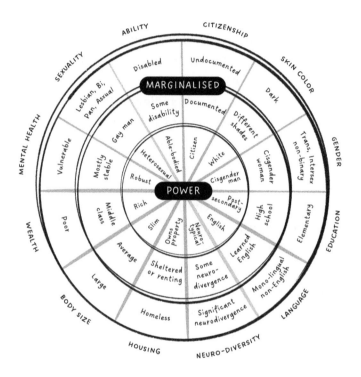

Figure 2: We all sit in different places on the 'Wheel of Privilege'. Try to make the exercise of seeing how your multiple identities are showing up and how they give you more power than others in society.

Taking various forms, privileges are related to gender, citizenship, skin colour, formal education, ability, sexuality, and many more aspects. With the hold of power comes the imperative to look after vulnerable citizens who might suffer from lacking privileges or support to advance their lives. In the meantime, there is a wealth of knowledge to receive from the ones making their journey without access to privileges finding a way to always be more resilient.

Today, we can clearly see how privileged individuals are overtaking power. The white, middle-aged, straight, educated male has become the default option for leadership. The discrimination of so-called minority[9] groups and the perpetuation of race stereotypes are an illustration of the non-acceptance of diverse identities by the system.

This situation reflects the domination of the Western European mindset on natural resources, the development of emerging societies, and the true expression of self. The privileged model of rewarding the powerful represents an inherited mindset of the mainstream culture that has been diffused through globalisation. While it has brought some positive aspects to the development of societies, globalisation has erased many forms of cultural diversity, identities, and heritages, influencing modern societies to look alike. The mainstream influence has led us to adopt a dominant attitude where our ego has become a driver for our loss of identity.

---

[9] *Minority is a perspective. A white European male is for instance part of the minority in Africa.*

HARNESSING EGO AND LETTING GO OF CONTROL

We have all experienced decisions we made that felt inappropriate afterwards. Often driven by our need for protection, we tend to react to protect what we have and who we think we are. This defence mechanism makes us believe that we must protect our identity using any means. In doing so, we miss opportunities to grow through new situations.

Our ego is the perception and consciousness we have of ourselves. The 'I' makes us think self-centred, with our ego often becoming our Enormously Great Obstacle[10]. Blinded by the 'libido of self', prioritising our instinctual energy and desires, we focus our behaviours on what benefits us, locking ourselves into who we are rather than who we could become. Driven away from our genuine selves and talents, we can be distracted from being our best, most authentic identity. This attitude comes from believing that taking risks is always dangerous. Stepping into the unknown represents the eventuality of losing more than what we already have and want to safeguard. The mainstream narrative tells us that it is always better to remain protected where we are rather than branch out for a more meaningful tomorrow. Relating to the privileges we have been granted or deprived of, this perpetuates a culture of the elite where the most fortunate remain on top of the pyramid shaping the lives of others[11].

---

[10] *Ego is the Enemy, Ryan Holliday.*

[11] *The Tyranny Of Structurelessness, Jo Freeman.*

Intertwined as part of the system, we have been made to believe that control could save us from risk and give us access to stability. This leads us to control others, nature, and things as if it could safeguard our position in society. We interpret it as if security came from protection and dominance over others that could represent a threat. Let's pause for a minute, asking yourself what you think of 'security', 'stability' and 'risk'. How would you define these three terms?

We all have diverse degrees of acceptance of 'risk' and needs regarding 'security' - while finding stability in very different situations. To reset the rules of the game, we need a new form of power[12] moving away from top-down power. The old forms of power, held by a few who are part of the dominant class, have enslaved our identities. Old power works like a currency aiming to capture and control attention, behaviours, and actions. It is not fit for the era we live in. If we want to revolutionise ourselves towards a meaningful future, we must become custodians of new forms of power. A type of power open for all, participatory and peer-driven, where one can help another. It is all about the collective, where 'we are because others are'. New power invites us to shift our identity, moving away from the 'I' and welcoming the idea that we have so much to gain in living the 'We'. It is about accepting that our identities are part of an interconnected web of life where we, alongside others,

---

[12] *New Power, Jeremy Heimans and Henry Timms.*

have a role to play in shaping our individual and common destiny.

By harnessing ego, we can enter a new sphere of life where our identity is sourced from the diversity surrounding us. Enriching ourselves from the world, we can enlighten our perspectives by accepting our connection to self, others, and the living world. This mindset can truly transfigure your existence, shifting from control to influence. It encourages you to set directions for your actions, beliefs, and interactions. It makes you accountable for establishing your way of honouring your complete identity. Your intentions become the driving force of your identity development. It is a malleable process where you grow into the person you are without wanting to dictate your path or how people around you should look or behave. You can accept to get rid of your frantic desire for control to live the 'We'. It will allow you to ask yourself what you can enable rather than what you can have or own. To reach such a degree of acceptance, you need to welcome emotions and vulnerability as part of your identity.

WELCOMING VULNERABILITY

The settings of our world reward power and dominance but do not leave much space for emotions. Driven by the frenzy of pretending rather than being, we are encouraged to build protection around us to show off. The rise of social media and advertising has created a bubble of moral correctness and forms of false positivity where being positive is perceived as the cornerstone of empowerment. It is one of the apparent examples demonstrating that individuals are searching for ways to build themselves into another identity in a virtual world. A way to escape the real now is to live in the illusion of something else—without solving the inner roots of our struggles. Such social networks represent the opportunity to create a new identity where anyone can be anything without having the accountability to share the day-to-day reality. All these modern norms perpetuate the standard of Western societies where being - or often pretending to be - strong and adverse is positively rewarded. A world where we are called to push emotions aside or ignore them. In doing so, we are cultivating the resentment of our past, amplifying our anger, pain, and sadness.

Avoidance and ignorance of emotions led us into a no-escape room. We are hooked on wanting to be 'ok'—ashamed to be and feel. The feeling of shame when expressing emotions comes from our fear of uncomfortable situations and vulnerability[13]. Feeling means opening up to let emotions come in and pass through ourselves. It means listening to our true selves without jumping straight into solutions but learning to deal with uncertainty. This is part of our social contract with life: being on Earth means taking life as it comes and living it with its ups and downs. What if life's beauty came from its intensity of emotions?

We need to recognise that the heaviness of certain situations is a call for personal development. By falling, we

---

[13] *Daring greatly, Brené Brown.*

learn how to stand up again and walk the path of life. Accepting pain, grief, loss, or regret gives us a greater chance of thriving. These teach us the way to resilience.

Radical acceptance of emotions is the cornerstone of a fulfilling life. Described as 'emotional agility' by Susan David[14], the commitment to feel is a commitment to live. In opening ourselves to be vulnerable, we can welcome a new range of sensations taking us to the next level of our identities. It is the doorway to living in harmony with our inner world. To learn how to deal with emotions is to learn how to love, care, parent and be in service to the future.

In making the step to feel, we leave space to be seen and see others. We open up a whole new world where empathy, compassion, and curiosity are helping us to spread into a better version of ourselves. The transition to being open about what we feel requires courage to face reality's adversity—accepting to be imperfect to birth new forms of love for oneself and others.

Seen as a weakness today, being vulnerable is undoubtedly one of the most critical strengths anyone can have. Accepting to be vulnerable is a spiritual awakening for a meaningful life. Living the moment, sensing the air that flows around us, seeing the looks of others, noticing the marks of affection we receive and give, and letting go of the judgements to welcome anything that comes our way. We are called to embrace the entire version of ourselves, accepting how we feel, look, love, interact and find joy.

---

[14] *The gift and power of emotional courage, TED talk by Susan David.*

KEY TAKEAWAYS

1. We tend to detach from our true selves to avoid resolving past issues and to hide behind a false identity that is supposed to protect us from harm.

2. We are composed of diverse influences and attributes, making our identities multiple. To welcome our numerous identities is to show the world how we want to be valued for our uniqueness.

3. Whether we have privileges or not, they influence our lives. With privileges comes the responsibility to be in service to those who did not have the chance to have them.

4. Our EGO can be our Enormously Greatest Obstacle, locking us into where we are, rather than how we could grow by getting rid of our fears and addiction to controlling our lives.

5. Vulnerability might be one of the greatest strengths of our time: being able to feel for ourselves and the living beings around us. We appreciate a deeper connection to the world by bringing empathy and emotions to situations.

PRACTICAL REFLECTIONS

→ Who is the true 'you' hiding behind your current perception of self-identity?

→ What does the social context around you prevent you from doing? How do race, gender or cultural stereotypes affect your life and daily environment?

→ How do you usually introduce yourself? Think about presenting yourself through what you believe, starting with 'I believe in ...'.

→ What if you could use your power to support a cause that needs more visibility and support?

→ How do you feel, and why do you feel like this? When was the last time you sat down with yourself to look at your emotions?

→ Inquire about what feels disturbing in your life that is blocking you from being yourself. What limitations do you face that are stopping you from advancing your existence? What is the emotion telling you?

→ Explore the wheel of privilege to see where you stand with your multiple identities.

CHAPTER THREE

HOW DO YOU BELONG?

—

'True belonging doesn't require you to change who you are;
it requires you to be who you are.'
Brené Brown

R aised in France, I come from a privileged background but without roots in one place. I never had the chance to experience a local community where I could rely on the local ecosystem to provide a sense of belonging. Nothing remains from my early childhood. Feeling rootless, my disconnection from place troubled my early life, causing a feeling of loneliness, lack of identity, and inability to rely on others. I thought I would forever have difficulty to belong. The struggles of my childhood carrying all the pain inside were too heavy to bear alone. But with time passing and new experiences, I came across two wonders that radically transformed my path and became my foundation for belonging. My approach to sport and nature has changed my life forever. It gave me the necessary resources to believe in the beauty of life and the role I could play in building the life I was meant to shape for myself and the world.

Sport has been the way for me to express myself without words, being in harmony with my body, feeling alive with painful legs, beating heart, and short breath. It saved me from life's struggles, providing me with hope, self-awareness and belonging. I found something in sports that I had never experienced before, giving me the hope that anything was possible when I was entirely motivated and committed. I felt my body again giving it life after a long hibernation that had cut off all my senses, closing me down into a dark space. Sport created a light inside me, calling for me to engage fully in life to feel that any effort would be rewarded by the same energy invested.

The practice of sport inevitably led me to outdoor spaces where I learned to be in synchronicity with the elements. From running barefoot in the forest to swimming in open water, I started noticing how my body adapted to weather conditions, other species, and the environment. I saw how calming and grounding it was to be in nature. I could hear, smell, and breathe alongside rivers, trees, and birds. These small and precious bits of life that used to be absent in my eyes became reasons for joy and fulfilment. I started to look at the world, feeling my emotions slowly and understanding how far I had been from the very essence of life. I opened up little by little, feeling a deep sense of belonging to nature and the world as a whole.

These two passions took me to new paths, leading my way with solo trips by bike or on foot, exploring myself and the world. It invited me to live in harmony with the environment, living with the elements and being humble to respect the power of nature above our heads and below our feet—staring at the stars at night, feeling the wind in my face, or listening to the sound of silence. These transformed me forever and are still part of my daily practices today.

In setting up new adventures, I came closer to the beauty of humanity, encountering an incredible range of individuals who were all bringing their magic to the world. I had become sensitive to life again and began to connect on a much deeper level with people. From strangers, people I met became allies. I could not list all my encounters, but a few will always spark a light in me, such as the one with Tigist.

While researching youth education in Ethiopia, the head of a local non-governmental organisation invited me to meet with his family, who lived in a remote community of forty inhabitants. It took us hours to reach the place, horse riding and walking in the magnificent countryside. I remember to this day the smell of nature and the peacefulness of the place. When we finally arrived at the community surrounded by bushes, I discovered an island of peace in the middle of nature. Faces brightened up, and instant human connections were made. After a few hours with the community, unable to communicate with words because of their local dialect, I felt a particular connection to Tigist. A person with whom we had no way of expressing ourselves but only gestures and looks to communicate. The smile illuminating her face and the lightness of her movements brought us into a state of peace.

The time we spent together taking care of the herd, cooking, and playing in nature remains part of the most memorable joys of my life. So simple and so real. The pleasure of connecting so deeply with someone without speaking a word. In there, I found the precious teaching that whoever we are and when willing to connect, our interconnection is here, waiting for us to welcome the relationships that can transform us forever.

Given my connection to sports, nature, and people I have come to understand that belonging is not necessarily about our geographic location but rather about being part of something going beyond ourselves. Something that can inform and guide our path in life as a guide rail for our existence. A powerful passion that can drive us well beyond the imaginable, creating new emotions and connection levels.

While many of us initially feel a sense of belonging with communities or groups, the root of belonging lies in our ability to belong as we stand for our core values and beliefs. True belonging is about being brave enough to inquire about our place in the world in relation to other beings and the living world. No matter how diverse our thinking and beliefs can be from others, we are all part of the same story—the story of life on Earth. Indeed, the politician, the local environmental activist, and the CEO of an oil company all belong to the same planet. Whatever their opinions, activities, and beliefs are, something bigger connects them all.

Belonging invites us to eliminate stereotypes and prejudices, removing barriers to interaction with our fellow citizens. It is about standing up for our convictions while building bridges to welcome existing connections between ourselves, others, and the world. It is an invitation to embrace differences and find ways of opening up new streams of thought where individuals can come together for something greater than themselves. We owe to be present with others to truly understand how we, the people, are writing the story of our time.

With belonging comes responsibility—the responsibility to acknowledge, understand, and honour our relationship with one another. We are called to recognise with great care that we are part of the same spiritual story and ongoing journey. As we embark on this path, writing the next chapter of humanity, we must rethink our relationships and interactions with life.

BEING IN RIGHT RELATIONSHIP WITH NATURE

The current economic model driving our world mad relies on the extraction and exploitation approach. Our economy is growing thanks to natural resources and people's work. We are damaging our home by depleting natural ecosystems to source raw materials and using cheap labour. The interpretation of our place on Earth was born from the capitalist narrative, leading us to believe that humans are superior to the natural world. The system spreads the idea that humans feel, think, and act while nature is an inert resource at our disposal. This has led us to violate nature by taking resources from the ground as if they were ours. From the fracking of the Earth to the extraction of oil, gas and ore, we are opening up the Earth as we would take someone's liver, heart or lung without permission.

The appropriation of natural resources accelerated radically with the advent of the Industrial Revolution. In need of so-called 'progress' to develop Western societies, governments and private institutions have taken control of the natural world. Nature is undermined. It became an economic opportunity, transforming forests into forestry, seas into fishery, and land into agro-business and mining. The equilibrium of life was broken with a massive push to extract value from the Earth.

In promoting such activities putting humans above nature, the system broke away from the emotional and cultural link ancestors used to have with their land. We disowned our link to the land hosting us to please the prerequisites of a system pushing us towards higher risks. The mainstream narrative created the common belief that nature was wild and needed restriction so that humans could remain on the planet. In a few decades, we severely damaged our essence of being connected to natural ecosystems. Wonders of the Earth, such as the great barrier of coral or the Amazon forest, have shrunk under the ever-growing pressure of human activity. Who knows what they will become in twenty years if we do not radically change our way of belonging and doing now?

The economic-driven model has led to tragic consequences we already experience, such as climate change or biodiversity loss. Today, humanity consumes the equivalent of 1.75 planets a year[15], with an exponential increase in the natural resources we use. From biodiversity to carbon emissions, the natural world suffers from human actions. Only 3 % of land ecosystems on Earth are preserved from their original form and, therefore, ecologically intact[16]. These significant impacts are taking us towards tipping points.

Understanding how we belong to our world is essential to reconnecting to what brought us and enabled our existence. We tend to forget that beyond borders, cultures, political opinions, and heritage, the planet is hosting us all. The single unit of life brings us all together under the same roof. We are one tribe made of life. Despite being nature, the mainstream story made us lose our sense of connection to the natural world and others. It narrates the story of disconnection, creating barriers to our relationship with nature and separating life into smaller, siloed elements. We have moved away from the deep integration of natural cycles and processes, detaching ourselves as if we were a separate entity of the living world.

This approach has created a collective trauma with a deep wound growing from disconnection. It has led us to

---

[15] *Earth Overshoot, 2024.*

[16] *Where Might We Find Ecologically Intact Communities? Frontiers, 2021.*

increased levels of fear, anxiety, selfishness, individualism and the obsession to consume to fill the gaps in our lives. From being hunter-gatherers, we have detached ourselves throughout history to become disconnected from the world and others. Given the legitimacy to act against forms of life, humans have built various systems of oppression, putting our energy against the living world rather than in service to its flourishing. It is time for the journey of reconnection: becoming more conscious and harmonious in our relationships.

BEING IN HARMONY WITH SELF AND PEER CITIZENS

In a world driven by the old definition of success, we tend to push ourselves forward without genuinely understanding the dynamics of our actions. We run after success as if there is only one way to reach the grail, a highway to the ultimate goal. Behind the current notions of success always hides the concept of the divide—a gap filled with violence separating humans from self, nature and others. Beyond our control over nature, we apply violence to people and communities. We have been indirectly encouraged to step onto others' feet, taking anything we can for our benefit. These multiple layers of disconnection have created some of the crises we know today.

The dominant approach that has exhausted nature also impacted social rights, with inequalities rising daily. Today, 81 billionaires own more wealth than 50% of the world population combined[17]. These crises all originate from the domination story. They are inextricably linked. It is as if the elite has developed, legitimised and banalised the divides to dominate the world by its own rules.

In this story of domination, the masculine-feminine stands as a clear example of the story of separation from self, others, and nature. Too often, women have been seen as nature, needing control to serve the cause of men. From this way of thinking emerged the promotion of masculine traits over feminine ones. Masculine attributes such as focusing on self, being competitive, assertive, or not showing emotions are rewarded. On the contrary, feminine traits such as showing compassion for others, being collaborative, being receptive, or exposing vulnerability are judged as weak. The classification of what is appropriate or not, based on a gender lens, sheds light on how our system is ruled by interpretation. This is like having a single perspective of men in a society designed by and for the interests of men. The reliance on domination has created divides with groups considered inferiors following the logic of colonisation. It has amplified the divide between groups, putting the most vulnerable at society's edge and taking away their dignity, rights, and opportunities.

It has made us adopt a perspective where we are encouraged to see everything and everyone as a resource. The default way we interact today is to extract something from most situations for personal gain. Many relationships

---

[17] *Survival of the Richest. Oxfam, 2023.*

are about consuming people as we consume products. We are often tempted to look for what people can bring to us rather than what we can reciprocally share. We tend to monetise relationships to expand our influence, status, or dominance over other social groups. With this mindset, the genuine connections that can transform our lives can become rare, impoverishing our existence. While the story is not over, and we still have the chance to reverse the process, our outdated approach to relationships has resulted in a disconnection from life. It has cut us down from the essential role of reciprocity.

As we transition towards the future, we must acknowledge these divides and move away from ignorance to reset our social relationships. This reset requires acknowledging the opposite and interconnected forces the Yin Yang concept illustrates. The Chinese philosophical model describes opposite but interconnected forces as being complementary. This is a reference point for us to understand how we can exist in relationship with the world and others. We all bring something unique to the world but cannot exist alone.

The Yin and Yang is the perfect metaphor to describe how our place in the world influences and is influenced by external forces that complete who we are. By changing how we see ourselves and accepting symbiosis with other life forms, we can welcome our complementary part to belong to something bigger than ourselves. Aware of our separation from nature and others, it is time to look at reconnecting with ourselves, too. To resonate is to give us a chance to vibrate again within the body that is ours.

RESONATING WITH LIFE

The acceleration of our lives has modified our place in the world. This decadent pace has led us to isolate ourselves from elements being part of our existence. Modern culture has conveyed the idea that empowerment is only possible through resources, creating the illusion of liberation and freedom for individuals, who gain autonomy by developing the image they have of themselves within the framework of society. This is why we often struggle to see the interconnectedness of our identities with what is around us, focusing our attention on ourselves. This has moved us away from reciprocity, indoctrinating relationships with the idea that there is an 'us' versus 'them'. This cannot be the way. We cannot just give or take. We exist through a greater sense of interconnectedness energised by a cyclical relationship with others. This is through mutuality and sharing that we build who we are as a person.

Our evolved relationship to life has transformed our connection with space, time, nature, people, and things. We have detached ourselves from the world, entering a form of alienation that has caused us to develop muted relationships with our environment. Our alienation came from the idea of acceleration, progress, and growth, losing track of our role as part of a broader system. We have developed a hostile relationship with the world around us and a disconnection of self—detached from our unique relationship with the living world. Suffering from the impossibility or inability to initiate a relationship with the world we inhabit. Imagine a mirror that does not reflect an image anymore. In getting used to taking more than we give, we have deeply weakened our ancestral link with life.

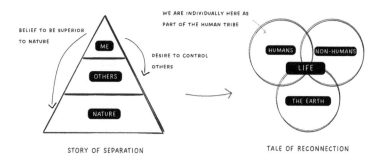

Figure 3: From the story of separation where we want to dominate, we can welcome the tale of reconnection. It is about understanding that life is about us as part of a wider system including humans, non-humans, and the Earth.

To move away from alienation and resonate again with the world, we need to understand how we belong to life. We are constantly connected to visible and invisible influences, shaping our identities along the way. Invisible strings influence our emotions, interactions, and feelings for one another. From our body sensations to our laughter, tears, and attention—all are languages shaping our identities.

Acknowledging and seeing these various forces can make us feel part of something bigger than us.

This approach of vibrating again with the world has been coined 'resonance' by Hartmut Rosa[18]. It represents our capacity to operate on a new level of interdependence where individual subjects respond and adapt to the world around us. The notion of resonance happens within space with a horizontal dimension referring to our social relationship with others, including romance, friendship or family; a vertical dimension referring to systems with a size more significant than the individual, such as nature, religion or art; and a diagonal dimension that illustrates our relationship to material things.

In all these co-existing relationships, resonance expresses how we can enable reciprocity and mutual transformation. By accepting to be transformed by elements around us, we let the world go through us, becoming a more fulfilled version of ourselves.

---

[18] *Resonance: A Sociology of Our Relationship to the World, Hartmut Rosa.*

KEY TAKEAWAYS

1. There are many opportunities to belong beyond place. To belong is to be in right relationship with ourselves and the living world.

2. The mainstream narrative of disconnection has taken us away from our core connection to nature, seeing ourselves separate from the living world.

3. In exploiting people and natural resources with an extractive mindset, we perpetuate tremendous harm towards life.

4. Our society has been built by and for men, discrediting feminine attributes. It has damaged the symbiosis of life, where forces are made to counterbalance each other.

5. We have become alienated by the system's drive for growth, progress, and acceleration, which has led us to think of our interests as separate from collective benefits. The key is to recenter our attention to the interconnectedness of our existences, supporting reciprocity in all we do.

PRACTICAL REFLECTIONS

→ How often do you spend time in nature? How could you dedicate more time to being outdoors?

→ How do you embed feminine attributes by showing compassion for others, being collaborative, being receptive, or exposing vulnerability?

→ How and when do you ask for support?

→ What attention do you give to life around you? Think of it from the food you eat, the people you cross paths with or the wildlife surrounding you.

→ What do you feel the most connected to? How can you explain the power of this connection? How could you develop the same relationship with nature, yourself and others?

→ How do you feel when you are in nature? Compare the ease you feel in your daily environment with your feeling in wild ecosystems.

CHAPTER FOUR

WHAT ARE YOUR NEEDS?

—

*'Earth provides enough to satisfy every man's need
but not every man's greed.'*
Gandhi

Cutting off from emotions shuts down our senses and misleads us when listening to our needs. I experienced this firsthand when I diverted my attention from what I could feel early on in my journey. I remember shutting down and being unable to listen to my deepest needs. By stopping communicating with myself, I did not accept to develop self-love and self-care. I transferred all my love and attention towards others, believing that being in service was the most significant endeavour anyone could pursue. I dedicated my daily activities to serving young people, vulnerable women, and deprived populations around the globe—leading impact initiatives to create healthier, happier, and safer environments for people and the living world to thrive. My commitment to serving others came naturally. I was pulled towards the ones in need putting my love, trust, and attention into others who were at a tricky point in life, trying to find ways to support them.

Years later, I unpacked my natural call to serve to clarify the place from where I was sourcing it. I realised that I was filling my needs gap by trying to help others to be fulfilled so that they did not face the situation that made me suffer in the past.

Like anyone, I needed to be loved and supported when things were shaky, and I never felt I had sufficient care. This left a deep mark on the person I became, and I unconsciously wanted to build upon my experience to share an abundance of care, love, and support for the ones most in need. I understood that all the energy I needed to receive was already within myself. I only needed to redirect some of it to bring it to my core. I learned how to listen to my needs and experienced the power of love and trust. In turn, this gave me much more energy to help others.

My situation was common. We are all stuck with our needs at some point in a world where we easily forget ourselves through the rhythm of collective madness. The mainstream model encourages us to look away from within ourselves. It diverts us from understanding what our basic demands are. We are used to rushing into the next thing we have to do rather than reflecting on what we truly need to feel in alignment with ourselves. Even our basic requirements, such as sleeping, eating or breathing, are relegated to the second priority. Many of us suffer from lack of sleep, eating disorders, or breathing deficiency, affecting brain and body functions. This stage of self-abandonment disrupts our interactions with the world, creating unprecedented levels of stress, aggressiveness, and sadness.

The accelerated accumulation of things and events blurs the clarity required to identify our deepest needs. Why should we question our needs when we are bombarded daily with multiple advertisements telling us what we want?

We are told we need the ultimate phone, the latest beauty product or the best travel plan. This detachment from our personal needs creates a gap in our personality, leading to biased choices. It takes us away from our identity and pushes away the love and relationships we need. We live like a sailing boat without wind, stuck in the middle of the ocean without the power to move in any direction. We must find our energy to move forward again, setting the sails towards more meaningful horizons.

Investigating our deepest needs is part of the beauty of self-introspection. It is the opportunity to know ourselves better and let our identity emerge from the noise of our formatted lives. It is a very personal inquiry that you are invited to lead to find the deepest patterns of what makes you fulfilled. Through lived experiences, self-confidence, and emotional agility, your unique self can unveil them.

Let's remind ourselves that needs are resources to take another dimension within yourself, to step up to the next level of your existence. It is something that has been within you, growing with experience. It is waiting for the waking time when you are looking for an answer to unleash its power to live a fulfilling life.

LOVING OURSELVES

The pressure put on the planet and people is proof of our disconnection to love—demonstrating our incapability to treat ourselves and the living world with care. It is directly reflected in us. We are squeezed into a role we have been asked to play without considering our unique attributes. This leads to mental health issues where we lose track of our role in society and the meaning of our existence. We drift away from our identities, cutting ties with our senses. It is like isolating everything that makes us who we are into an airtight box and living a life ignoring this part of us. It creates aches and pains that express our abandonment of self-care and self-understanding.

Living by individualistic standards, we still need to understand how to look after ourselves. We have diverted our attention from our beings, leaving our uniqueness behind. We have created layers of complexity in our lives by moving away from our true identities. The detachment from self stretches our lives, leaving little room for self-care and love. But reclaiming this space is essential. How can we love and do good for others when unaware of what fulfils us?

The way we relate to our identity and self is an excellent indicator of how we energise ourselves with the strengths required to move forward. Unfortunately, we tend to neglect the importance of looking inside and listening to our internal voice. This voice often tells us we feel pain, struggle with something or lack attention. But the external noise catches us up to run away from the truth. Sitting down with our thoughts and emotions can be extremely helpful in identifying our internal callings. To turn our attention to love is a great way to look after ourselves. It can give us a perspective on one of the most critical drivers of fulfilment. Love can set us free.

To look after ourselves is, first and foremost, about inquiring about the love we are giving to ourselves. Indeed, while modern society speaks most of the time about love in relation to romantic relationships, it goes well beyond that. Too often, love remains a gap filler rather than an enabler. As Bell Hooks[19] wisely shares, we have been made to believe that romantic relationships 'will rescue and redeem us' from our affective gap. The hope of love saving us cannot work as it is a passive attitude towards something we expect. On the contrary, love must be an active, voluntary and spontaneous way of being with everyone. It amplifies life experiences to gain confidence in experiencing and interacting with the world.

Paying attention to love transforms it into an enabler. For this, we need to go back to its origins: ourselves. Love is not something tangible but an element of who we are. It is an energy floating in our lives that we can decide to grasp or let go of. We produce it constantly and have it within us. The main challenge leading to our detachment from it is that we all have suffered in one way or another from affective gaps. Not receiving the attention we were expecting, we tend to create a defensive mechanism aiming to have control over love. We are trying to make it tangible

---

[19] *All About Love: New Visions, Bell Hooks.*

by opening up or closing its gates—believing we can master it. The reality is that love cannot be controlled. It flows through us. We make it alive with our looks, gestures, words, and actions. It is a multidimensional aspect of our lives, interconnected with all parts of ourselves and in relationship to everything around us. When acknowledged, love quietly living within us can be awakened. In the inquiry into feeling and sensing love, trusting ourselves can allow us to get closer to our needs.

TRUSTING OURSELVES

We create constant competition through direct and indirect stimuli. From the advertisements we see every day to social media and our relationships with others, we are constantly triggered to compare and compete. Becoming the norm, we continuously try to weigh ourselves in relation to others. 'I' versus 'them'. This phenomenon has moved our reference point from who we are to who the mainstream expects us to be. We have replaced our self-trust with the false recognition of societal standards. It has led us to believe that we must reach these standards to be accepted as part of the system. By adopting these modern ideals, we have slowly given up on believing in our capacities to be. Putting futile attention on the superfluous hope for self-realisation. In doing so, we are shrinking our identities—triggered with the message that we are not enough.

Societal norms have standardised what is good and evil. It has created multiple layers of shame and developed a feeling of inferiority. The pressure we put on ourselves to fit the standards makes many of us adapt so as not to be perceived as different. This develops shame in ourselves and the way we are. When seeing the crowds following the same path, many wonder if they are 'thin enough', 'rich enough', 'beautiful enough', 'smart enough' ... and so on. It makes us wonder, 'Am I being enough?'. We fear the disconnection from the masses in doing things our way and being ourselves.

In deforming our identities to please others, we lose trust in our capabilities to bring something unique to the world. We develop patterns of inferiority with phenomena such as the impostor syndrome. We doubt our skills, abilities, or values with an internalised fear of being a fraud. We feel out of the game, considering ourselves insufficient for the competitive standards. The anxiety sitting within ourselves keeps on being fed as we interact with the modern world. Competition recharges our resentment towards self and others using us to self-sustain the never-ending comparison cycle.

Driven by our need for recognition to feel supported in advancing our lives, we want to be heard, seen, and validated. Taking our independence with the decisions we make, the opinions we have, and the values we defend can help us get a greater sense of realisation—without the need to get immediate recognition. It can give us the independence to shape our thinking, acting and being.

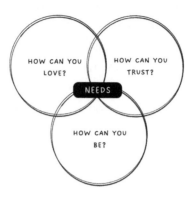

Figure 4: To listen to our needs, we need to inquire about the way we love, trust, and are—with ourselves and others.

Staying true to who we are is about trusting ourselves and living our lives in the way we believe is most appropriate. No one other than yourself can tell you how to live your life. Having the courage to stand up for your identity and beliefs can lead to fulfilling your needs and understanding that you are more than enough.

We are invited to understand that being is not about ticking boxes of what others expect from us but about bringing your whole selves to the world. If life has been given to you, it is to live fully, taking ownership of how you want to exist. Leading your way can give you a sense of agency, helping to eliminate the demons that make you doubt and embrace the role you can play for yourself and the world. It can direct you towards the next version of who you can become.

EMBRACING THE NEXT VERSION OF OURSELVES

Being filled with love and trust for who we are and what surrounds us is a powerful enabler to spring into the next version of ourselves. It helps us shape a solid foundation for building a thriving existence in right relationship. This attitude towards self and the world can enable us to step into a new paradigm where all our internal energy can become the driver of the new direction that is calling us.

Nevertheless, the current system keeps us away from listening to our dreams and ideals. It constantly convinces us of the difficulty of making them happen. It tells us that any dream is a utopia making us believe that it is more reasonable to think within the framework of what already exists. We have this voice from the outside constantly telling us not to dare to make radical changes in our lives, risking too much of the gains and stability we may already have. Whether it is about changing our jobs, evolving within a relationship or changing the place we live, it makes us fear change.

This vision makes us feel that dreams and life changes are risky and unrealistic. The narrative puts us down and takes us away from what we have the potential to become. It boxes us into a field as if we were settled forever without any evolutionary perspective. It makes us choose to stick to the status quo, not listen and comprehend the callings we have. This sense of security in the future is misleading. From our jobs to our relationships, these can end from one day to the next without warning. Even life can vanish in the blink of time. This is part of the beauty of life we are invited to welcome. Being present and trusting what the future will bring us. It can radically help us move from shrinking to expanding our identities. While we should give importance to living in the present, we can intensely focus on what direction we want to head towards—valuing our dreams and unleashing our curiosity.

By welcoming anything that comes your way through the lens of intention alongside deep attention and care, you can make every experience a learning opportunity to get closer to the next version of yourself. All your life circumstances can help you get closer to your aspirations, foreseeing your future identity as you portray it. You can be in tune with the world, accepting it as it fuels your soul. We all need to dream of what tomorrow could be like, with a sense of direction. The need to envision the future we desire is within us all.

You can ignite your internal energy by revealing the direction of travel you want to follow. The sense of perspective is not about the outcomes you want to achieve but rather about the ideals you wish to pursue. It is an aspiration to reach higher, once unimaginable latitudes.

KEY TAKEAWAYS

1. The consumerist system has created needs that supersede our personal needs. The constant noise surrounding ourselves leads us to make inappropriate choices in how we live our lives. Having less but being more is the direction we need to head in.

2. Our liberation will come from removing the costume role we have been given, replacing it with the complete and accurate version of ourselves: loving the way we are and showing up to the world.

3. We all need to be seen, heard, and validated. The system uses it to make us compare and compete. We should cease deforming our identities to please others. We are sufficient the way we are and should trust ourselves in following our gut instincts to live our existence responding to our needs.

4. Because society has constructed the so-called 'failure' myth, we often remain scared to listen to our callings. We should dare to trust our abilities to make our wildest aspirations happen. We have been given life to live fully. Nothing should stop us from making our dreams come true.

5. Given our current model, we have evolved with a false sense of security. Anything can end without warning. What we thought we had established yesterday could be an old memory tomorrow.

PRACTICAL REFLECTIONS

→ What personal needs should you fulfil to thrive? (financial, well-being, social, creative, cultural..., etc.)

→ How do you ensure that you keep some time to listen to your inner callings, paying attention to your personal needs?

→ What is essential for you to feel at ease and thrive? How do you reflect on what connects you to others and the natural world?

→ How do you distance yourself from the stimuli you receive every day from advertisements, social media, and society?

→ When was the last time you felt at ease showing up with your true self to others?

→ How much are you influenced by peers, marketing messages, and society in the way you are? Think about how you dress, speak, identify, love, feel, hope, desire or even expect.

→ What do you aspire to become? What are you dreaming of that could unleash your real personality?

PART 2

MAKING SENSE OF THE WORLD

Following the self-introspection, it is time for us to understand how our culture, education, and privileges influence how we see the world. In an era of globalisation with the standardisation of our lives, it is our responsibility to be critical about how we interpret the world around us.

The second part of the book invites you to explore how you shape your opinions, live a more conscious life, and respond to the current crisis of uncertainty. Once again, it encourages you to challenge some of your preconceptions of the world and take a step back to see what you might have taken for granted in the way you pursue your existence.

Making sense of the world requires an openness to novelty to accommodate diverse visions of what the world can look like, depending on where we sit at this moment in time. Let's explore how the world is unveiling and unravelling.

CHAPTER FIVE

HOW DO YOU PERCEIVE?

—

'The question is not what you look at, but what you see.'

Henry David Thoreau

I have always been amazed by how talking to diverse people could highlight the divergence in our worldviews. Meeting people from various backgrounds, political opinions, and trajectories made it clear that our perspectives reflect our experiences. I gained a significant understanding by listening and interacting with people from different paths. From policymakers, homeless people, migrants, unemployed youth, factory workers, and wealthy investors, I got the chance to understand how different our languages can be. Behind these labels, I saw deeper patterns of struggles, traumas, and hope in all these individuals who often do not speak to one another or speak a different language.

Hungry to keep growing the number of glasses I could use to see the world, I started exploring various places and fields with the burning desire to experience novel perceptions, emotions, realities, opinions, and aspirations.

Living with a Western mind, I realised how biased I was in looking at the world, understanding that our realities are only part of a bigger reality. From the 'monoculture of the mind'[20], I opened myself to an incredible range of people, and each encounter brought something new to reinvent my way of seeing the world. This eagerness to discover with active listening and understanding might have been the most beautiful gift of my life. It taught me so much to this day that it became a motive to keep going towards others, be curious, and empathetically try to understand where people are coming from. While I lived the diversity of perspectives, I also understood that there was no need to go around the globe to see the difference in how we think and interpret the way society exists. Our reality differs from the one of individuals living around the corner of our street. We interpret the world based on many aspects such as education, life events, or privileges.

A few years ago, I started inviting random people I would meet in the street to grab a coffee, realising how much there was to share with strangers. Always starting with eye contact, this practice often led to fantastic conversations, connecting on many levels and enriching my diversity of perspectives. I also made the practice of hitchhiking a habit —being picked by random citizens crossing my path. I recall this unforgettable journey in the Italian countryside of

---

[20] *The cultivation of one mainstream cultural movement where many elements of our lives have been standardised. It influences our lives from the food we eat to the movies we watch, and the activities we do.*

Tuscany, wanting to head to the beautiful town of Pienza. After many train delays and cancellations, I convinced myself that the best way to arrive at my final destination was to stand on the road catching a car. The experience was much more insightful than planned, with five different vehicles taken and twelve individuals encountered in less than sixty kilometres. Beyond the travel, the journey has been about the people who, one after the other, opened up about their lives and vision of their place. From parents driving their kids to friends going for a day trip and couples heading home, they all had a unique perspective. I ended the journey with a toast at the house of the couple who picked me up for the final stage of the journey. We shared time at their place, speaking for two hours while playing with their daughter and enjoying simple moments of life.

Beyond the hope provided by the kindness and openness of all these people to pick me up and connect, I was deeply enriched by the diversity of their perspectives. Each of these discussions led bits and pieces of their vision of the world to emerge and show how it could become a better place. They all had something to say, with diverse ways of seeing society.

This example illustrates how our life experiences become our truth about how we see the world, often ignoring the various perspectives surrounding us. We are often locked into a unique reality of ours. From stigma to racism, citizens have created misconceptions of others by not knowing them. We have excluded some groups for their attributes, creating a divide that is fatal to many underrepresented groups suffering from discrimination for centuries. As Ruth Wilson Gilmore[21] described it, racism is the premature death of differentiated groups discriminated against for their characteristics. Our responsibility is to take ownership of the injustice to heal our complex relationships with the past.

There are multiple truths about how to see the world. All are valuable and can enrich us. Despite their importance, we all tend to perceive through faulty lenses, missing the complete picture. The complexity of seeing the world as a whole comes from the importance of understanding and accepting the multiple factors that have influenced how society has evolved. If globalisation has led to the standardisation of the world as if there was only one truth, our collective story is much more nuanced. The standardisation of our lives across the globe has often erased the authenticity and uniqueness of places, people and history.

By spreading a monoculture of the mind, societal rules have transformed our lifestyles and made citizens part of a single story where no room was left to question our collective past. We came to the world inheriting a legacy of human suffering, fears, and profound traumas that are still very much part of how the world operates. From our survival instinct to the Western European colonisation in the Americas, Africa, Asia and Oceania, and the wars happening across the globe, we all carry this part of history within us—

---

[21] *Ruth Wilson Gilmore is a prison abolitionist and prison scholar.*

whether we are on the perpetrator or victim side of it. These scars have been influencing our perception of reality. We need the courage to dive deep and uncover these hidden truths to build the future. We must heal our collective history to eliminate the outdated patterns that still rule our lives.

MOVING AWAY FROM THE SINGLE-STORY

The way our society has come to dominate nature and individuals is inspired by our heritage of colonialism. Colonialism is the structure through which one dominant group subordinates and exploits another using a justification for this to happen. The dominant model has ruled the world for centuries. From ancient to medieval times, colonialism has evolved into the 'Age of Discovery'[22] and to the most recent form called 'New Imperialism',[23] where the Western world conquered most countries of Africa and parts of Asia. This process has been about taking control of a piece of land and a group of people inflicting terrible damage on human lives and nature. Powerful

---

[22] *The Age of Discovery was a period largely overlapping with the Age of Sail, approximately from the 15th century to the 17th century in European history, during which seafaring Europeans explored, colonised and conquered parts of the globe.*

[23] *New Imperialism characterises a period of colonial expansion by European powers, the United States, and Japan during the late 19th and early 20th centuries.*

countries have taken ownership of others to benefit their economic interests.

From producing goods with local resources to using individuals to create workforces, countries enslaved people and parts of the world to grow their domination. The model that is now part of history books has left its print in our daily lives with the way we still think, operate, and perceive. These social beliefs have created a way of life with a heritage in the way we see and think about race, social class, culture, gender, and sexuality. Intertwined with the model of colonialism, the model of patriarchy expanded in the Western world as the dominant way of being. It refers to a system of society in which the masculine holds power, essentially excluding any other form of identity and therefore creates unbalanced power relationships.

These divides created decades ago are still ruling our unconscious. Meanwhile, the power dynamics between countries still perpetuate a form of colonisation, with countries in the North still controlling the South with debts, political influence, and cheap labour production. We even see the growing trend of countries buying land in other countries to access water or strategic resources—often at the cost of communities. This model is part of the obsolete system we live in, where the ones in power control the ones who have been subject to colonisation in the past. Creating the ambivalence of power and playing around with the notions of scarcity protects the status quo of the dominants. It manipulates us and nature for the benefit of the system to retain its dominance. The toxicity of history remains anchored as part of our identities, and many of us are not yet ready to recognise the inconvenient truth.

The denial of such a situation leads us to see the world through a single-story lens. A vision that occults the legacy of our past and how collective memories influence our lives. The monoculture of mind we experience is presented through the lens of the Western perspective. It took away the different points of view and lived realities of people who have experienced diverse situations and often suffered from oppression. This unidirectional perspective creates an incomplete view influencing our interaction with the world.

Our role is to open our minds and hearts to welcome what the world has to say, operating our metamorphosis of perspective. Zooming out from our micro reality to see the interconnectedness of our histories, opinions, and shared beliefs can help us gain wider perspectives. It can enable us to move away from stereotypes to welcome the richness of diversity and understand our system's underlying patterns. As Chimamanda Ngozi Adichie[24] puts it: 'Stories have been used to dispossess and to malign, but stories can also be used to empower and to humanise. Stories can break the dignity of a people, but stories can also repair that broken dignity'. The story of humanity is fluid with an incredible array of perspectives. It is up to us to reconcile different stories to multiply our sources of understanding.

---

[24] *The danger of a single story, TED talk by Chimamanda Ngozi Adichie.*

UNLEARNING TO GET RID OF OUR BIASES

Everything in life is a matter of perception. Nothing exists until it is interpreted. This leads us to use glasses from everything we've seen and experienced. Our unidirectional vision of the world results in biases in how we think, speak and belong. This personal perception brings us to delusion, where what we believe to see seems to be the reality. We all have a confirmation bias that makes us stick to those with similar ideas and shared beliefs. We find reaffirming sources rather than confronting opinions when searching for information. Look at the newspaper you read, the social media accounts you follow or the friends you have. Most sources around you are probably sharing ideas supporting your existing beliefs. Bias makes us become part of virtual echo chambers where people thinking alike gather based on their shared visions.

From your political opinion to your interest in a specific topic, you are part of sub-groups that amplify your thinking biases. These social groups operate as separate bubbles evolving in a parallel world. The agreement becomes the main priority, sticking to the ones sharing our opinions so that we feel part of a supportive social group. This like-minded effect represents a massive limitation when growing beyond our perceptive borders. It makes us ignore the diverse realities and prevents us from confronting ourselves with divergent views.

There is something to learn from everyone we encounter and any new situation we face. Having the humility to listen and reflect on what others have to say is a significant step in moving from a bias of perception to a broader spectrum of life perspectives. By offering the opportunity to immerse ourselves in diverse realities, we can grow our awareness of the multiple layers of life. It is like putting on various lenses one after the other to be able to zoom in and out, seeing from right to left and from bottom to top. Evolving from inadequate perception to the multiple realities of the world, we move to a greater degree of perspective.

Many of the things we pretend to know are personal interpretations we have made of a situation. As the majority rewards knowledge as power, we are not driven to question our understanding but rather to stand for it in front of others. The true wealth of knowledge lies in lived experiences where one has lived different lives by immersing oneself in various contexts and challenging assumptions. Welcoming new experiences can take us to unexplored horizons we could not have imagined before. It can take us to a broader picture of the richness of life, encompassing more of its aspects.

This thinking invites us to move from knowing as a static state to embracing a place where we can rethink and unlearn to transform ourselves. There is so much we can gain from the discomfort of not knowing. It can leave space for new knowledge to transform us. Not knowing is a beautiful aspect of life, as it allows us to grow with the help of others in various situations. It invites us to open up to divergent opinions and confront ourselves with alternative truths—being reminded that we are often tempted to favour the convenience of conviction over the uneasiness of doubt.

Nonetheless, true friends or allies will not always agree with you but make you reflect on where you stand in the world and how you can see beyond your reality. To grow, we need situations that require adaptation and resilience to come up with new answers. Multiplying these experiences is essential to make us think hard about what we believe to move beyond our perception and welcome the wisdom of perspectives.

MULTIPLYING WAYS OF EXPERIENCING

To observe and experience is to change. Through lived experience, we can get the most beneficial insights about the meaning of life. Seeing the world through diverse angles allows us to become the custodians of a thriving future. To do so requires a new mindset, welcoming novelty with an open mind and heart. A mindset that goes off track from the conventional way of thinking distributed by the mainstream media and narrative. Looking only for like-minded peers should be over as it makes us run out of the collective intelligence we can gain from unlike-minded encounters— with people who differ in their way of thinking, being and experiencing.

Let's face it: we tend to suffer from homophily[25] with beings around us thinking the same way. This is why we greatly need cognitive diversity to bring openness to our

---

[25] *Homophily is a concept in sociology describing the tendency of individuals to associate and bond with similar others, as in the proverb 'birds of a feather flock together'.*

lives and innovation to our world. True diversity is represented when people from multiple horizons collaborate to discuss, imagine, and co-create. It creates what Matthew Syed[26] calls 'the wisdom of the crowd', where the wide diversity of views fosters the emergence of a much more elaborate outcome. Imagine talking about the meaning of life with a group of people who come from diverse places, have various levels of education, disparate economic resources, divergent political opinions, distinct aspirations in life, and different hobbies. Collective intelligence will help each participant gain a bigger picture of realities while enriching the conversation's outcome.

To experience the presence and views of others is already a significant step forward. From our differences can emerge a profound wisdom. Bringing these differences to life is an incommensurable asset for us to grow through the wealth of experiences and visions. Cognitive diversity is at our doorstep, waiting for us to welcome it. Going out and talking to any 'stranger' can do the work. Why don't you go to your neighbourhood and speak to the first person you meet?

People might be a few metres away from where you hang out, but miles away when it comes to how they see the world. This practice enables us to see what we have always taken for granted in ourselves and confront realities to gain insights. Seeing ourselves and the world through a fresh and multifaceted perspective, we can rethink our lives and feel the world around us. It invites us to empathise with others,

---

[26] *Rebel Ideas: The Power of Diverse Thinking, Matthew Syed.*

putting ourselves in their shoes and gaining insights into their lives.

To sense and let our minds wander during these experiences can become a real asset in paving our way towards a greater understanding of realities. Practise active listening without preconceived thoughts or expectations, letting the person take you to their world and travelling alongside them into unknown ideas.

All this is about accepting to put ourselves in movement again, gravitating amid viewpoints and bringing vulnerability to tap into our intuitive, emotional, sensory, and rational forms of knowing. By getting to know realities, we flourish into a more informed version of ourselves, which helps us to welcome the new with humility and openness. It liberates our ability to imagine new stories for our lives and the future we want. In the meantime, it can change us profoundly from within by giving us the means to live a much deeper life experience alongside others. Our new experiences can liberate our intrinsic motivation and inspire us to celebrate uncertainty, be open to possibilities, welcome cooperation with others, and act on the stories we want to write.

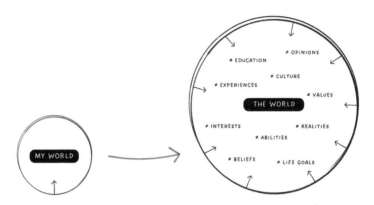

Figure 5: From YOUR world (a mono-perspective vision), you can embrace a wider perspective of THE world. To immerse yourself in new environments, with different people, and in new cultural contexts can provide you with transformational insights.

KEY TAKEAWAYS

1. The mainstream model has developed a monoculture of the mind where we are all encouraged to think alike. Globalisation has led to the standardisation of reality, putting one story together for us and tempting us to erase the authenticity of places, people, and history.

2. The single story has locked us into one perspective reality, often corresponding to the dominant Western view. We need to welcome diverse voices so that we can be critical towards our perceptions, opinions, and vision of society— healing with our heavy heritage of colonisation and exploitation of communities from the Global South.

3. Our perspectives need to comprehend the full range of citizens' collective views. Immersing ourselves in unknown circles helps to eliminate our preconceptions of reality. Exiting the bubbles can help us discover new horizons and confront everything we interpret or take for granted.

4. One of the main opportunities of our time is to unlearn. It is to reappropriate the world through new experiences rather than old prejudices and judgmental perspectives.

5. Cognitive diversity is the way forward to co-create holistic perspectives of what tomorrow could become. When designing new pathways for humanity, we should invite everyone to the table.

PRACTICAL REFLECTIONS

→ How do you spot monoculture patterns and distance yourself from them?

→ How do you pay attention and do your part to heal the Western heritage of colonisation and support a system in right relationship with the South?

→ How do you challenge your perceptions and ensure you overcome your biases?

→ How do you enrich your perspectives and welcome a multidimensional story?

→ When was the last time you spoke with a stranger? How could you make it a practice?

→ How would you see the world if you were ... a homeless person living in the streets of your neighbourhood, a refugee fleeing the war and arriving in your town, a person victim of sexual abuse, a child suffering from mistreatment, a billionaire living from its rent, a cashier in your local supermarket, a person coming to life in 20 years.

CHAPTER SIX

HOW CAN YOU BECOME
MORE CONSCIOUS?

—

'Forget your voice, sing! Forget your feet, dance!
Forget your life, live! Forget yourself and be!'
Kamand Kojouri

Haunted by my demons for many years, I filled up my days with many things to keep running away from my core. I was convinced that living my youth at its best was to be hyperactive with dozens of projects, always planning the next thing. Focusing on what was next made me rush in life, always living faster, missing out on the opportunity to be present. I was following the trend of being in the infinite hamster wheel, turning into circles without genuinely appreciating the singularity of each moment. From entrepreneurial initiatives to sports, I was always called by the next thing to do, focusing on getting things done but never slowing down to live at a human pace. I was attracted by the adrenaline rush of doing more. It was like a drug that would take over my life, dictating my moves and pushing me constantly to do more.

My wake-up call came from seeing how our addiction to speed brought us closer to the edge with the multiple challenges of our time. I received an inner calling inviting me to change myself first to co-create tomorrow's world. I realised that to lead change, I first needed to make a change in myself, encouraging others to follow the same path. I understood that shifting our consciousness was the first stage towards helping others to build a more conscious version of themselves and, therefore, enable change through conscious individuals rising.

In this journey, nature has been a critical driver in helping me reconnect with cycles and flows. From seasons, moon cycles, tides, or rivers, I sourced inspiration by spending time in the wilderness, seeing how rhythms stabilise life on Earth and so can ground ourselves. Already driven by the idea of slowing down, I crossed northern Europe by train a few years ago, heading to Norwegian Lapland. The journey took me several days and many stops, allowing me to encounter new people and appreciate the value of time. After weeks of travel, I arrived in Alta, 400 kilometres north of the Arctic Circle, where I lived for several months in wintertime. Beyond the privilege of this choice, I enjoyed the magnificent experience of polar nights, extreme cold, and wilderness. I settled with the firm intention of wanting to be in tune with the ecosystem and myself being forced to adapt to the context where nature dictates the rhythm of life.

Not seeing the sun for more than eighty days but only pink and blue skies for a few hours a day made me realise how we can take what nature provides for granted. My daily walks in the dark, with some strong winds, snow, and temperatures reaching minus thirty-five degrees Celsius, put me in a state of humility I never experienced before. I was inspired by nature's beauty and rawness, feeling so little in the immensity of wilderness still untouched by humans. Many times, tears of gratefulness came to my eyes. The pureness and peacefulness of the experience moved me.

I recall this encounter I made on the 24th of December on a morning walk, ending up face-to-face with a reindeer in the local forest. First intrigued by my presence and therefore wary, he kept a certain distance and forced me to stop to respect the space between us. After long minutes of observation in the cold, I decided to continue hiking. A few minutes later, I realised the reindeer had started following me with a magnificent elegance. We were two living beings in the wild walking together in the snow surrounded by pine trees, deeply connected. With this powerful experience and a firm intention to slow down, I became even more conscious of the elements, being grateful for experiences, relationships, and life itself.

While I struggled to transition to adopt a slower lifestyle through the years, I quickly understood the benefits of living in a much deeper connection with myself and others. I decided to give up on the superfluous and focus on the core, welcoming the idea that it was possible to do less but better. In doing so, I could have a much more significant impact on the cause I was working for. Directing my energy better towards what matters helped me find balance with myself and the world. It offered a radical change in my presence on Earth, aligning with my mission of serving others to find their inner peace.

In paying attention to people's attitudes towards life, I saw a familiar pattern of busyness. We constantly rush to follow the dynamic to gain, collect, and succeed. The rhetoric aligns with our system: always faster, bigger, and more, with eternal acceleration. As human beings, we became 'busy beings'.

'I am so busy these days and do not have time'. I would bet that you have heard it a hundred times and may even have said it yourself. It became a buzz(y) word—a must-say to show up as being in action in a world constantly increasing speed. We all want to be part of this busy tribe without acknowledging its toxicity. It has become the norm, and everyone is following the trend as a mimetic driver, automatically excluding those who might want to slow down. This is because the individual definition of success has been built upon the idea that busyness equals worthiness. Having a packed agenda and showing up as busy gives a feeling of importance and accomplishment. It validates our existence. The use of never-ending to-dos is an escape from our realities.

But the truth is that collective hurry leads us to a societal catastrophe where individuals are fuelling the obsolete system against themselves, denying their needs, and becoming part of the herd. The meaning of being busy is to be enslaved by time and lose balance with ourselves. It means letting external elements manage our lives and losing our sense of identity by being too occupied to think, question, and be. Time is taking us away from living a meaningful life where we can be conscious of our needs and listen to our callings. To move away from the frenetic noise around us is to liberate ourselves from the burden of time to prioritise what truly matters to us. What if tomorrow was the last day of your life? Would you live the same way and choose always to run faster?

Aiming for balance is not easy, but if everyone were to slow down, we would live in a much more balanced society, reconnecting ourselves to the essence of life. The time has come for us to reclaim our power, give meaning to our lives, and contribute to the birth of a new world.

EMBRACING OUR WHOLESELVES

If we are buying into the system of busyness, it is mainly because we are feeling more comfortable running away from our demons than embracing the reality of our lives. We keep ourselves busy to avoid doing the self-introspection we need to be at peace with who we are and how our life looks. Because we are spiritually empty, we fill ourselves with things to do and have. It makes us crave more, never conscious of the present moment to enjoy what is. The psychological state of endless craving becomes an addiction, making us forget ourselves. We are always focused on the next thing we will do, the next person we will meet, or the next stuff we will get. We are locked into the obsession of feeling occupied looking away from the mirror of our lives.

Being brave enough to slow down, reject societal pressure, and do less is liberating. Slowing down invites us to live in the present moment, removing the noise that pulls us towards what could come next. As Eckhart Tolle shares it, 'The present moment is all you ever have'[27]. It should be cherished to move away from what we have to who we are, living in tune with the now. It is to welcome gratitude and be thankful and appreciative of what life is. From the people we meet to the moments we experience, it is essential to recognise any single joyful moment as being content with the simple act of being. To welcome gratitude is to accept and welcome life as it is, taking it all. It is an invitation to welcome its circumstances without losing energy or ignoring what you used to run away from. What was part of your life yesterday will remain until you address it. Only true dedication can help you overcome the challenge.

We are invited to make the necessary shift from seeing challenges as opportunities for growth to adopting a radically new mindset of acceptance, where you become proactive about solving what needs your attention rather than escaping it. It is like having an injury and choosing to keep on running. You can try to keep running forever, but at some point, your body will need to pause to recover. The way to go is to slow down, have the courage to face

---

[27] *The Power of Now: A Guide to Spiritual Enlightenment, Eckhart Tolle.*

challenges and enjoy finding a way to heal your pain. From this stage of healing, you will gain clarity over your life with a beautiful sense of relief being consciously present.

It is like welcoming and uncovering our new identity from layers of noise, pretension, and shame. We have to mourn our unconscious selves as they were to birth our authentic and conscious character, nurturing what is yet to come. As Carl Jung[28] puts it, 'Until you make the unconscious conscious, it will direct your life, and you will call it fate'. The work on our unconscious requires us to accept and let go of the old to welcome the new. It helps us understand that letting something die is to give space to new forms of life. This is tough for us to accept as many of us have been raised with the idea that death is something to fear. Nevertheless, death is the precondition of life and is present in all processes on Earth.

To live in resonance with the world, we need to accept letting our old self die making space to welcome the new. This consciousness shift allows us to focus our attention on what truly matters, vibrating again with the elements around and within ourselves. To reach such a level of awareness, you can invite yourself to move away from being busy to being fully present, embracing the moment.

_____

[28] *Carl Gustav Jung was a Swiss psychiatrist and psychoanalyst who founded analytical psychology. Jung's work has been influential in the fields of psychiatry, anthropology, archaeology, literature, philosophy, psychology, and religious studies.*

TRANSITIONING FROM BUSYNESS TO PRESENCE

The rapid river of our lives takes us away from what truly matters. It makes us travel too fast to really understand our existence and fully grasp the meaning we want to give our path. We are constantly urged to do the next thing, concluding we do not have time. There is never enough time to see our loved ones, share quality time with others, sit quietly on our own, or even be gentle with ourselves. It feels like time is sand running out of our hands.

But by taking a step back, we can realise that time is not something we do not have but something we do not take. It is often our deliberate unconscious or conscious choice to run short on it. We are depriving ourselves of living purposefully following our values and aspirations, preferring to sprint after the expectations we put on ourselves. This is symbolised by the Greek words 'kairos' and 'chronos', expressing two definitions of time. 'Chronos' describes the seconds, minutes and hours we find in clocks and watches, while 'kairos' stands for deep time with special moments where the world seems to stop, such as a deep breath, a magic sunset, or a profound look. 'Kairos' stands for qualitative time, helping us to move forward with transformational moments. It is the time we desperately need in a world running too fast.

When taken away by the million things we need to do, we drift so far away that we shut ourselves down to exist through the spectrum of 'chronos' time and expectations we or others project into us. This makes us live our lives far from the true essence of what life should be about.

Transitioning from busyness to presence is the way to reclaim ownership of our lives, taking responsibility for making time for what matters to us as a deliberate choice. Being present means living in the moment without always making a plan. It means welcoming moments of boredom to let our minds create and innovate. It means living spontaneous moments where emotions and feelings carry us gently. It means being thankful for what comes our way and fully welcoming what is. It means providing ourselves with the luxury of writing new stories from blank pages.

By setting the intention of making time for ourselves, we can take a significant step towards a state of flow, welcoming the way life comes to us. Taking time is allowing yourself to wonder, feel, contemplate, connect, share, reflect, experience, explore and so much more. All this can open up a new chapter of your life that will not look like anything you have ever experienced.

It is our mission to break the chains of time enslavement. In doing so, we can find a new way of being that is free from what used to overtake our liberty of living. It can help us regain influence over our lives, be open to our true selves, and explore what being present means. By refocusing your attention and channelling your intention towards things that matter to you, you can open a new chapter where all your time will be transformed into energy you can invest in setting yourself in motion.

Making time for ourselves goes beyond our well-being and happiness. It can radically change our role in the lives of others and the world. Taking time means being more attentive to peers and what surrounds us by welcoming our senses to feel what is happening around us.

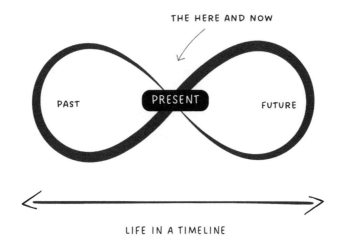

THE HERE AND NOW

PAST PRESENT FUTURE

LIFE IN A TIMELINE

Figure 6: In between the past and future is the here and now. This is a gentle invitation to live in the present moment looking after yourself and what surrounds you now.

To slow down and be present is to open our eyes to where we live and what is around us. From the sound of birds to the faces of others, all the details we used to ignore finally appear crystal clear to us, making us alive again. We can finally pay attention to the people, demonstrating empathy, love, and kindness. We can help others by seeing them and creating the stimuli that encourage them to see us. We can also start to listen to the silent cry of the natural world in need of respect and acknowledgement for its fragility from the harm human beings perpetrate.

We live in a critical era where everything always goes faster, and the sense of urgency to respond to crises is growing. But in times of crisis, the biggest mistake would be to act too quickly. As Bayo Akomolafe[29] says, 'Times are urgent, so let us slow down'. To slow down will have ripple effects on how the world stops being driven by acceleration. To choose presence over busyness is to initiate a meaningful path towards a healthier future. Don't rush; the choice is yours.

DOING RIGHT FOR OURSELVES AND THE WORLD

Many believe that being busy is not a choice but something we must accept. Nevertheless, busyness has been created in our society to divert us from what matters. It is possible for anyone committed to making the conscious shift of slowing down to make it happen. We can all reduce our actions by choosing what we genuinely care about. Make a list of what you do daily and review what truly matters; the result is often surprising.

Today's reward is too often about quantity over quality, with society rewarding the production of junk stuff over what brings quality into our lives. Look, for instance, at your cupboard and the incredible amount of things you have

---

[29] *Bayo Akomolafe is an author, celebrated speaker, teacher, and intellectual whose vocation goes beyond justice and speaking truth to power to open up spaces for new thinking.*

acquired that you may have used only a few times. Would you instead go for the quantity of stuff piling into your life or the few but meaningful events that can awaken your soul? Minimalism gives us greater satisfaction, valuing what surrounds us and who we are.

The current model of mass consumption encourages us to run after the accumulation of things, social relationships, and activities as if they could fulfil ourselves and facilitate our emancipation. Today's mental health crisis, with many of us collapsing under stress, burnout, and loss of purpose, proves it wrong. Under social pressures, we waste an incredible amount of time checking the next thing we could buy, how many likes we get on social media, or watching senseless content distracting us from the presence of our lives.

The overvalue of non-essentials is noise, diverting us from the core of what is truly important and neglecting the enriching experiences life can bring us. Replacing all these moments of deviation with some free space can radically change our lives. To take time is to decide what to prioritise and align with the meaning we want to give to our lives. Anyone can access this level of freedom, where choices can become determinants of using time wisely. Greg Mc Keown[30] speaks about shifting from the 'undisciplined pursuit of more to the disciplined pursuit of less', insisting on the need for essentialism to become our compass in life. What if you could do less but do it better—following your heart? This

[30] *Essentialism: The Disciplined Pursuit of Less, Greg Mc Keown.*

goes through the understanding of what must be done, what is nice to have, and the rest. If you do not prioritise through decisions in your life, others will decide for you.

Selecting what truly matters in your life and picking the main elements enabling your happiness, sense of security, and self-love is critical. Making a list of all you do and eliminating all the superfluous can already make you feel like you have gained so much freedom. It can help you remove obstacles in your life where things used to feel like they could not be reorganised and reordered.

In this endeavour, learning to say 'no' is a great help to move away from constraints and make space for what feels genuinely suitable. It can protect you from always doing more—sensing that when it is not a clear 'yes', it should become an obvious 'no'. Trading off things to do in your life for personal space is the best way to clean up the endless list of things you could do to focus on the essentials. You will soon discover that it will give you power again to say 'yes' to what truly matters.

Being conscious that choices are yours and that you can reclaim the trajectory of your life is essential to succeed in the transition. Overwriting today's reality with what tomorrow could be is a powerful driver for you to support your personal transformation and do good for the world. If everyone were to do less but better with a slow pace of mind and action, the world would be better today.

KEY TAKEAWAYS

1. From human beings, we became 'busy beings'. Busyness is the construction of our minds that encourages us to always be faster and have more while perpetuating eternal acceleration. The craving for gain makes us lose track of our lives.

2. Being busy is about being enslaved by time and rules, compressing our identities into what is expected. It deviates from who we can become, setting ourselves on the path of alienation.

3. Time is not something we have; it is something we take. In doing less but better, we are given the possibility to make decisions for ourselves. We can prioritise what truly matters.

4. Our demons are here and will only become allies once we do the work of understanding them and finding solutions to their causes. When facing problems, we should dedicate the right resources to solve them. Let's not postpone the essential work.

5. Being conscious of ourselves is the best way to make the world conscious. To become aware of who we are is also to help others find their true light and path towards consciousness.

PRACTICAL REFLECTIONS

→ What is urgent and essential for you?

→ If you had one day, month, or year to live, what would you change in your day-to-day life?

→ How often do you use the word 'busy', and what does it mean to you?

→ When looking at your daily habits, what do you do that truly matters? What brings joy to your life? What puts you down or triggers a feeling of disconnection from yourself?

→ How do you feel when saying 'no'? How often have you said 'yes' to others in the past months when it did not feel right?

→ Write a letter 'When I am gone'. What do you want others to know about how much you love and care for them? Please share it with the ones you care about to show your appreciation.

→ Book time with yourself during the week to be with your thoughts and emotions and reflect on your journey. You will see an increase in consciousness.

CHAPTER SEVEN

HOW DO YOU THINK LONG-TERM?

—

'We are on Earth to take care of life.
We are on Earth to take care of each other.'

Xiye Bastida

I started my journey focusing on serving others, thinking that environmental issues could wait to be resolved later. I got alarmed by the many wildfires, floods, and sea rising events happening around the globe, wondering about the influence we, humans, had on Earth's systems. Called back by the urgency of the situation, I learned about how our presence on Earth had disrupted natural ecosystems to unprecedented levels, putting our lives and those of the generations to come at risk. Deep diving more and more into the subject and understanding the madness of our behaviours towards nature, I was caught in action. I thought of the life I could have in fifty years and the existence of children if no change was happening. I realised my responsibility to give the Earth the care and attention it deserved—giving back what life had gifted me. I understood that a healthy environment was the critical condition for life on Earth, meaning that our ecosystem was interconnected.

This was a complete shift in my way of seeing myself being in service to people in need at this moment in time, to being in service also to the ones to come. I understood that considering the following generations was a more significant way of solving the problems at their root rather than covering them with quick and urgent plasters. Working with decision-makers significantly impacting the lives of populations, I saw firsthand how the most deprived were left behind the curtains of power. The system unveiled in front of my eyes with profit, power, and privileges being the main priority for the 'powerful' preserving their status rather than fostering social and intergenerational justice—to support the ones most in need.

In the meantime, I experienced multiple waves of hope connecting with vulnerable individuals, helping to move our collective. From young people living in deprived neighbourhoods to dedicated changemakers bouncing back from life events, I found an irresistible power in people coming from underserved communities with high hopes and the capacity to make things happen. It inspired me to change my way of living and to think differently: constantly zooming out. I learned that by looking behind the boxes surrounding problems, ideas, and solutions, many other alternatives are available. Putting myself in the shoes of the living world helped me make better decisions. To see the world on behalf of someone living in another part of the world, someone who will be born in 50 years, or the perspective of natural elements such as forests, oceans, or animals can truly shift the way we live.

This practice invited me to think outside the box and make decisions focusing on a long-term perspective. In taking a guardian role to protect what can still be saved, we can learn to give back so that the next generation can live with positive credit rather than debt. Thinking of debt is not something our society recognises as it rewards short-term gains. Imagine a kid having gifts and wanting to open them all as fast as possible. We are driven to rush into everything we can take rather than recognise the importance of balancing for tomorrow. This attitude has detached us from how we define value and honour the advantage of what we have around us.

We have been encouraged to have a quick return on our investments, detaching ourselves from time. This has made us addicted to the immediate gratification of taking and having, losing a total sense of where resources are coming from, how relationships need time to develop, or what heritage we can leave for future generations. It has all become about what we can get now rather than how we can collectively collect the fruits of our existence with a vision going beyond our personal gain. This mindset principally comes from monetising all citizens' resources and actions to fuel indicators such as Growth Domestic Product (GDP), which calculates how much value a country produces within a year. This economic referential has led us to become financial value producers in the short term, forgetting how essential it is to create different forms of value such as well-being and happiness. In following the mainstream of short-term profits, we are on course to overthrow Earth systems, widen the divide between individuals, and jeopardise our common future. The reality invites us to reposition ourselves at the right place in time. It encourages us to rethink our position in time to adopt a higher level of consciousness where we understand how our presence on the planet results from many generations before us and that our passage into the world is also something future generations will inherit. Taking the perspective of a human, a tree, or a whale, what is a generation?

As we face tremendous pressures on Earth systems, we must rethink our place in time with humility, acting from a place of stewardship. It is a call for us to embrace our given role as guardians of the future. Let's stop borrowing from our children.

REDEFINING THE NOTION OF SUCCESS

Thinking long-term is first about challenging how we define success and value. Today's lens makes us see the world as if the only determining factor of success were in economic terms. From the salary we get at the end of the month to our designated social status, we have been told that the monetary value we create and accumulate can tell how successful we are. Look at all these books telling you how to 'get rich' or these ads telling you how to 'look great'; they all sell what has been told is the dream of a lifetime. Based on their message, there is no other option than being a winner or loser. Either you follow the common dream, giving up on your aspirations and fitting into the system, or you will fail and be excluded. The dualistic vision of our lives makes us judge ourselves and others based on criteria designed to support the obsolete system.

To be successful in that sense can often be harmful to others and the world while making us unhappy. No wonder the ones considered to be the most successful entrepreneurs today are the ones who have built tech empires or extractive businesses. Success goes hand in hand with the frame of the way our capitalist world sees the importance of domination. Who are the real heroes of today's world? Are they the Musk, Zuckerberg, and Bezos? Or the Attenborough[31], Goodall[32], and Mandela? It is now the time to honour the emergence of local heroes who take ownership of their lives and lead change in their local communities.

In taking over lives, resources, and the future, the so-called 'successful' fit with the old narrative, driving inequalities and injustice forward. This very egocentric and competitive definition implies a win-or-lose position for citizens. It has led us to the challenges of our times with an inadequate framing of what the world needs to return to a hopeful path towards a just future for all.

As we witness the loss of many forms of life, we need to stand up for a new way of defining success by considering life as the priority. We need a new vision of success that embraces all aspects of influence one can have on society. A

---

[31] *David Attenborough is a renowned broadcaster and biologist.*

[32] *Jane Goodall is a renowned primatologist and anthropologist.*

comprehensive approach encompassing how we can positively contribute to life on Earth. We need to reset the rules of the game, unleashing a new paradigm where individuals are invited to be successful considering the positive impact they can have on society. Think of all these people giving their time to support just causes. The value they create in caring for others, giving back to their community, or preserving natural ecosystems is often overlooked. This is where the key lies for us to move from the old to the new. We must find meaning in the value we bring through our existence to leave the world in a better place than we found it. Behind each of our lives lies the potential to do good. What does success look like for you?

To choose to be successful in futuristic terms is to give back more than we take. It is to create opportunities for others, regenerate ecosystems, spread love, enable opportunities and empower ourselves to live the great reset. We all have the power to start our own journey of redefining what success means to us and how we can create value on our terms for the world. What if your power was not only in what you can do as an individual but also in your ability to be part of a collective going beyond your generation?

We urgently need to write this story to unleash new imaginaries of tomorrow's indicators. From destruction to regeneration, economic growth to quality of life, and injustice to equity. We have the opportunity to co-create a new paradigm. Being humble enough to do our bit and dedicating ourselves to living purposefully can make miracles and a positive difference beyond our lifetime.

BEING A GOOD ANCESTOR

We will be on this planet for a couple of decades, taking the relay from previous generations and giving it to the ones to come. Holding the baton of life, we have the duty to pass it on in a better shape than we received it. As the famous Native American proverb says, 'We do not inherit the Earth from our ancestors; we borrow it from our children'. This perfectly expresses the intergenerational transmission between our existences, showcasing that our lives are part of the bigger picture of human life on Earth. To accept this responsibility we have received is to access a new perspective. It is to acknowledge how our behaviours, beliefs, and attitudes can influence the course of history and humanity.

Today, eight billion of us are alive, just a tiny part of the estimated hundred billion people who have lived on the planet. Many are yet to come. If they are given the conditions to live, they will look back on us and the legacy we leave them. Imagine arriving on this planet with debts and burdens from previous generations. To be just with the generations to come, we need to move away from all the blockages affecting our addiction to short-termism.

As described by Roman Krznaric[33], short-termism is fuelled by the tyranny of the clock with busyness and rush, digital distraction with our attention hijacked by technology, political presentism with a focus on the next election, speculative capitalism with volatile markets,

---

[33] *The Good Ancestor, Roman Krznaric.*

networks of uncertainty with increased risks and pandemics, as well as perpetual progress with endless growth perspectives. We must meet the task of intergenerational justice and not fail to provide the next generations with their core needs.

From these limitations, we can evolve to unleash our ancestral thinking and being to lead with a long-term mindset. This is the antidote to the challenges we face and the future we can unfold. Stepping into an ancestor role, caring about the legacy we will leave for future generations.

We must remind ourselves that we are all visitors to the Earth. We are adventurers in this time, place, and era. We are passing through. Every one of us is a blink in the light of history on Earth. Therefore, our role as guardians is to observe, listen, learn and preserve intergenerational knowledge. We have so much to learn from the elders and indigenous people who have lived guided by ancestral knowledge and can teach us how they lived in equilibrium with life for centuries. Being a good ancestor requires us to be humble about our limited time on the planet, welcoming our fragility. It invites us to be in tune with the world around us, resonating with others and the world to make decisions that favour the deepening of our place in relation to the world.

To step into this new role, we need to accept uncertainty, transform what we used to consider challenges as opportunities and find our unique contribution in service to the world. We should invite ourselves to challenge our preconceptions of the future to accept that we can shape history by making our societies more resilient and flourishing. From this place, we can leverage participatory and collaborative power to co-create the change we hope to see in the world. Being vulnerable in adversity can uplift us by empathising and feeling for what surrounds and transforms us.

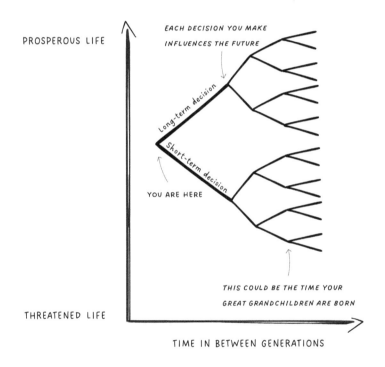

Figure 7: Daily decisions influence our future and the one of the generations to come. For our great grandchildren to inherit a liveable planet, this is up to us to adopt a long-term thinking mindset.

In becoming the guardians of the future, we can be in tune with the natural world and others making the right decisions for sustaining life on Earth. The Seventh-Generation Principle[34] can guide us on the journey, following the idea that any decision we make today should still have a positive and lasting impact for seven generations ahead. We must ask ourselves what kind of ancestor we want to be, giving back to life and fully honouring the responsibility given to us as citizens of the Earth. Adopting a stewardship mindset will give us a more grounded perspective, allowing us to let our imagination and actions drive a hopeful future.

HOPING AND ACTING FOR WHAT IS TO COME

Everything goes too fast. We see the world moving at an incredible pace, unable to grasp its changes and evolution. This sense of emergency has led us to live in stress, wanting to make quick decisions or distance ourselves from the world. As we take on the relay for generations to come, the question is whether we want to let future generations inherit a stone or a feather. The choice is in our hands to leave a burden or a springboard for them to live meaningful lives.

---

[34] *The Seventh Generation Principle is rooted in the age-old wisdom of the Haudenosaunee (Iroquois) people, which advocates that the choices we make in the present should ensure a thriving and sustainable world for the next seven generations.*

Seeing the world the way it looks today makes many wonder what is still to save, considering the chaos we have made. But in cracks always appears light, inviting us to imagine what tomorrow could be. As expressed by the beautiful Japanese word 'Komorebi', there is always sun leaking through the leaves. Imagine yourself walking in a forest and feeling the early sun rays of the day warming up your face. This is the light that always remains. We are invited to welcome it to gain perspectives of the future we desire. The fate of our species and existence has yet to be written. It is where the importance of sourcing energy from hope is, taking us closer to tomorrow's possible reality.

While optimism is about seeing the bright side of life in a passive sense, hope is truly about having active ideals where our commitment takes us in an unexplored direction we are shaping for ourselves and others. The story of hope is a call to imagine, going outside the frame that has created today's crises. As Buckminster Fuller[35] puts it, it is not about fighting the existing reality but building a 'new model that makes the existing model obsolete'.

Hope is a fantastic enabler in creating new narratives and imaginaries, letting go of our limitations and welcoming possibilities. To hope is to be ready to welcome the future with a fresh perspective, giving us the agency to act upon strong ideals. In hoping for a better tomorrow, we can unleash the power of long-term thinking, building our

---

[35] *Richard Buckminster Fuller was an American architect, systems theorist, writer, designer, inventor, philosopher, and futurist.*

vision around the idea of onboarding generations to come into collective dreams of making change happen. It is about setting a firm intention and creating a vision about something we want to see happening in the world. Echoing the powerful words of Jane Goodall, 'what we nurture and encourage wins'[36].

As we face unprecedented challenges, we have to hope, imagine and make what tomorrow could be. The process of hope requires us to accept the possibility of not succeeding. It requires us to set clear and inspiring objectives depicting the reality we are designing with ways of making these goals happen. With a specific dose of realism, one is invited to believe that these goals can be achieved and receive social support to continue fighting for the vision in the face of adversity.

Being hopeful is our duty to act on the injustices and crises of our time. It means recognising that a problem requires attention and action, realising that tackling it is the only way to go. Hoping means acknowledging that the risk of not acting is greater than failing to solve the issue. For this reason, hope is our engine to face society's failure and bring a fresh perspective of what could be tomorrow.

To nourish hope is to give ourselves and future generations a chance to live in a new model that genuinely honours the legacy transmitted from generation to generation. An approach that does not see generations as

---

[36] *The Book of Hope: A Survival Guide for Trying Times, Jane Goodall, Douglas Carlton Abrams and Gail Hudson.*

separate periods within time but rather as bridges to foster intergenerational knowledge and wisdom nourishing the ones to come. In bringing intergenerational knowledge to the story of hope, we can become the relay runner for future generations, holding the baton that will make us collectively win the battle for a better future.

KEY TAKEAWAYS

1. In times of crisis, thinking long-term is the antidote to ensure intergenerational, social and environmental justice. The times call on us to think beyond our existence, providing future generations with thriving life conditions.

2. We need a new definition of success with new forms of value where one can be encouraged to do good for the planet and communities. Beyond disconnecting us from our motherland and humanity, the race for short-term profits is making us crash the world.

3. Each of us represents a blink in the history of the planet. We will be on Earth for a few decades. We need to approach our role with humility, realising that our existence is due to previous generations and that our actions will influence future generations.

4. We are the guardians of life's fragile equilibrium. While the planet does not need us to survive, we need her to sustain our species. We have the moral duty to transmit the relay to the next generations with a better world state.

5. Hope is a powerful and active tool for projecting ourselves into possible futures. Imagining the future in 50 or 100 years can help us create new ideals, encouraging us to make them happen so that we and the next generations thrive.

PRACTICAL REFLECTIONS

→ If you could speak to your ancestors, what would you ask yesterday's inhabitants of the Earth to do for you to have a better life today?

→ If you were born in 50 years, what would you ask today's inhabitants of the Earth to do?

→ What does success look like for you, nature, and future generations? To what extent are you prepared to challenge the conventional understanding of success and outcomes?

→ How do you welcome emotions and foster empathy with future outcomes in mind when making decisions?

→ What are we to each other on the planet? What are we to the generations that have given us life? What are we to the generations that will come to life after us?

→ What kind of ancestor do you want to be? What contribution would you like to make to your generation and the ones to come?

→ What dreams do you have for humanity's future? How can you initiate the journey to make them happen?

CHAPTER EIGHT

HOW DO YOU EMBRACE UNCERTAINTY?

—

'Life is about not knowing, having to change, taking the moment and making the best of it, without knowing what's going to happen next.'

Gilda Radner

Conflicts and crises make our existence feel like we are on the brink of something new and threatening every day. I often felt overwhelmed by the world's state and still feel its weight daily. From climate research showing our tragic course towards immense risks to conflicts spreading around the globe, the daily news weighs heavy on us. We are inundated by successive happenings mounting our fear to see the next extreme weather event, pandemic, or war hitting us home. The instability of the situation encouraged me to develop greater resilience to accept the uncertainty of our lives, welcoming any sudden change rather than going against it. The reality invites us to remind ourselves that change is part of our lives and that we cannot control everything.

Looking back at the process of welcoming my fears alongside the complexity and uncertainty of the world we live in, I have gained tremendous confidence through the stories of remarkable individuals who have been able to respond to life-changing events. I have a particular thought for Farnad, this young Afghan boy I met a couple of years ago in a refugee camp in Athens, who naturally opened up with me sharing about his journey to reach Europe. His story, alongside many of the dozen stories I heard from people going through various tragedies, told me so much about how we define uncertainty based on our experiences.

For him, uncertainty had reached its peak when he made his way leaving and crossing war zones on his own at the age of thirteen. He had no choice but to trust unknown people to bring him to the next stage of his journey before heading on an inflatable boat in the middle of the sea betting his life to live in a peaceful part of the world. Despite the uncertainty of his past journey and future in a new land, he embraced life by welcoming anything that came his way. He dreamt of becoming a ballet dancer to inspire people. His life journey demonstrated the power of human resilience.

People like Farnad have awakened my soul, inspiring my perspective on uncertainty and risk. I realised that to accept not having control over the future is liberating to enjoy the present moment. The lack of predictiveness in our lives encourages us to learn how to surf the waves coming our way. These waves result from the complex nature of our minds and relationships with the world, with the construction of a society that has created multiple layers of complexity. We live in an era of high volatility, uncertainty, and ambiguity, where all the parts and variables of our lives are intertwined. While our knowledge of life, thanks to science and personal experiences, is constantly increasing, we still have so much to learn and many elements out of our hands. The many crises unfolding are taking us to a new level of uncertainty, with increased variables creating unpredictability in our lives. What if we were learning to surf on uncertainty, navigating fluidly?

Some significant events shaking the world could be on the verge of happening. Whether we speak of pandemics, conflicts, or climate disasters, we must consider their eventual occurrence. As we approach tipping points with Earth's balance and face the deepening of social crises, we must deal with a future that cannot be set in stone. No one can predict what tomorrow will be like. Would you even want to know?

The uncertainty, linked with the perceived complexity of our system, frightens many of us, activating our immune system and provoking strong emotions. Many wonder about how the world will look in ten or thirty years. It is like losing ground below our feet, plunging into the emptiness of the future. There are multiple directions we could be taking as a society. All these changes in our equilibrium of life will reshape our world to its new phase and reshuffle the cards of society and, therefore, our lives. It will invite us to adapt to new conditions of life, resetting many of the standards we have had until now.

Consider that our natural reaction to unpredictability is to shut down to create distance from the perceived risks and discomfort provoked by the situation. It makes us behave in an individualistic way, often cutting us off from the reality of the world, which we then begin to deny or avoid—think of human responses to climate change for example. Rejecting all forms of resonance, we erect virtual walls, shutting down our emotions and relationship with the world, believing that this virtual shell will protect us from the risks ahead. The anxiety, anger, and fear rise as we cannot externalise our emotions.

The truth is that we cannot evolve into a wiser version of ourselves as long as we are driven by fear. As Baptiste Morizot[37] suggests, we are encouraged to practice 'negative navigation' when not knowing where we are and what is yet to come. Inspired by sailing techniques, it is a way to be safe while navigating in unknown places. When we are lost, the most important thing is to know what the danger is and to do everything in our power to avoid approaching it. By using the unknown as our compass, we can navigate our uncertain and unpredictable lives.

As the times call us for more coherence in our lives and societies, we need to learn how to become more resilient, accepting the fragility of life. We need to move away from our self-defence mechanism to a more welcoming state where risks are fully integrated within who we are and how we operate—accepting to get lost to find our way.

---

[37] *Ways of Being Alive, Baptiste Morizot.*

WELCOMING THE EMERGENT

We are complex beings by nature with countless emotions, feelings, and attributes, making each of us unique. Our self-portrait is complex to realise as we evolve and are influenced by the world around us. It keeps on shaping who we are, how we think, and towards which horizons we are heading. The mainstream narrative pushes us to the extremes of control to make us feel we are in a safety zone by conforming to the system.

But life cannot be controlled, not even by the system. Every single element that makes up life contains many parameters that can change over time. The indoctrination of being safe and stable by having a house, a family or a car takes us away from our true nature of living in reciprocity with the world as it surrounds us. It encapsulates us into a false sense of security where our only ambition is to secure what we have and focus on safeguarding our virtual walls of supposed protection and stability. Our fast-paced world is changing daily to evolve into the next version of itself so why wouldn't we also accept this emergence by letting ourselves flow with novelty as events come through?

We need to ask ourselves whether or not we want to keep playing it safe, manipulating our whole perception of life to feel secure. Moving away from our virtual refuge where we shelter ourselves. This refuge is often nourished by self-satisfying actions in our day-to-day routines, not aiming for anything new or challenging. We put ourselves at even greater risk by cutting us off from living.

This invites us to realise that to be alive is to accept the fact of dying. It is to acknowledge that our existences are made of thousands of events that will influence the course of our experiences, hundreds of encounters that will take us to new roads, and dozens of chapters that will take our lives towards new horizons. To live is to feel energy coming to and from us, responding to the world. Life is not and will never be a quiet path. It is what makes it beautiful and invites us to move away to welcome the emergence of what is yet to be.

Going out in the wild and quitting our virtual shelters can be life-changing. It can enable us to free ourselves from all the prerequisites of false security and servitude to expectations lying over our heads. Truly feeling the world is to get out of our so-called comfort zone. Stepping into the wild paves the way towards liberation, with a new world opening up. In awakening your senses, you can give space for the novelty of experiences and sensations to emerge. It is the opportunity for you to welcome new questions - moving away from quick solutions to inquiries - wondering about what tomorrow could bring. It invites you to be patient with everything that sits within yourself. As Rainer Maria Rilke[38] wisely suggests, you are invited to 'be patient towards all unsolved in your heart and try to love the questions themselves to live the questions now.'

In welcoming emergence, you can access a new mindset that positively approaches what is coming your way,

---

[38] *Rainer Maria Rilke, Letters to a Young Poet.*

welcoming uncertainty and becoming increasingly resilient in responding to any new situation in life. It can unleash your adaptability to live in harmony with the world as it presents, having an open state of mind and being ready for any turbulence you might encounter.

NAVIGATING THROUGH CONFUSION

Our lives can seem messy, frequently adding up on top of the confusion of the world we live in. The growing noise takes a lot of our precious energy, diverting us from what truly matters. These confusing stimuli often create anxiety making us feel lost in the middle of many signals. It disturbs our clarity and deepens our uneasiness to be in tune with our need to make progress in our journeys. This often takes us to a breaking point where we feel lost in the vast ocean of unknowns.

This confusion adds up to our growing addiction to the zapping culture which has made us reach the point of what Gérald Bronner calls a 'cognitive apocalypse'[39] with lower levels of concentration. While we have gained considerable 'brain time', we are overwhelmed by a cacophony of sounds, images, and stimuli capturing our attention. The digital revolution and rise of social media information have denatured our minds and revealed the deepest essence of the human tendency to be absorbed into the din, alienating us through fear, anxiety, and often anger. The path we collectively take has diverted our attention to oversimplified

---

[39] *Cognitive Apocalypse, Gérald Bronner.*

facts, escaping situations that could lead to confusion and disorientation. We have buried part of our abilities to break apart from challenging times, forgetting the importance of inquiring for self-realising purposes.

When facing confusion, we often try to run away, thinking that avoiding the challenge will take us to a more serene place. We are formatted to separate from reality instead of connecting with it, pulling back rather than welcoming, and closing down instead of opening up. This mindset is like taking a pill to solve all problems. Until we reach the roots of the issue, it will resurface and keep us in a confused state.

The fear of losing control with confusion is a natural reaction to getting closer to the truth within us. It is a course-direction insight that takes us towards the right track for ourselves. When disoriented in our life path, we can seize the opportunity to reset our way of doing and thinking to find new points of reference that will take us to the next stage. To find our paths, we must accept getting lost in the process, welcoming what society would call failure as a strength to get us closer to the answers we seek. The process should not be about trying to cure the discomfort immediately but rather about sourcing its causes and better understanding how it can take us further in our journey.

It is essential to listen to our inner voice and follow our intuition to explore our inquiries, setting up a path to clarity and resolving confusion. The importance lies in the process more than the answers. It is to live the experience of inquiry that takes us further in life, being flexible enough to spring into a new version of ourselves. As Bayo Akomolafe says, we should learn to 'dance with the unknown'. This is the way for us to learn how to be okay with confusion and gain insights as life takes us on a bumpy ride. The perceived chaos of life events is a calling for us to dive deep, taking the time and putting our attention to better understand where we are heading. It is a teaching that helps us to understand that uncertainty and confusion are essential ingredients for us to rise. To move away from our incapacity to welcome confusion is to open new doors to unexplored roads that will lead to a more authentic life in balance with the welcoming of who we are yet to become.

TRANSFORMING FEAR INTO ACTION

Our minds are running many miles per hour, constantly predicting what will come our way. Bombarded with negative news and toxic information, we are continually triggered to imagine the next catastrophe and how it could affect us. The spread of buzz news triggers our cognitive system to create apprehension about what tomorrow could bring. This narrative corners us into the room, fearing the multiple hypothetical challenges that could affect us. Using our common beliefs and anxieties, the fear narrative makes us lose track of ourselves trying to plan the escape from problems that do not even yet exist. Digging deeper into the root of fear, we can realise that it comes from scenarios we are making up for what could potentially happen.

Looking for solutions to something that hasn't happened yet, we exhaust ourselves by cultivating a growing fear of what might happen. We try to put potential problems in front of possible solutions, but most of the time we don't have the answer. All this creates the fear of facing challenging moments that could attain our identity, beliefs, or existence. Our intolerance to uncertainty takes so much space in our lives that it directs away our energy towards the feeling of fear rather than the welcoming of possibilities. There is not yet an event that our mind is already working on suggesting that something negative could happen in the future. It always takes us away from living the present fully.

Fear is nothing else than a construction of the mind. We are intimidated by what could come up in our lives, having a passive attitude towards what we could suffer from. In creating dark possibilities, we direct our energy into feeding negative thoughts rather than focusing on taking action towards acting upon uncertainty. Nevertheless, fear can become a healthy driver when apprehended with the trust and courage to transform its perceived negativity into a positive force taking us forward. In fear lies an immense power to lead our lives towards better futures. As Nelson Mandela once said, 'I learned that courage was not the absence of fear, but the triumph over it. The brave man is not he who does not feel afraid, but he who conquers that fear'. The courage to face our fears is crucial for us not to be limited but energised by anything that might come our way.

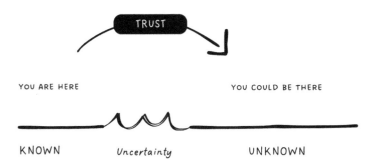

Figure 8: Trust will be your greater ally to transform fear into action. Making the jump to unknown areas of your life will be scary but always rewarding.

Mayan and Amazonian indigenous cultures have always used the metaphor of 'touching the jaguar' to symbolise the courage to overcome doubts, challenge what we face, and overcome obstacles. Their wisdom encourages us to go out there to identify our fears and dare to confront them by accepting their existence and taking action to change ourselves and the world. It is an encouragement to have the audacity to welcome what scares us and get over it through understanding, acceptance, and action. To live fully, we need to let go of our deepest fear through the love of living. Facing the fear of dying can, for instance, give us a strong sense of living. To see the brightness in what is yet to come can strongly influence our relationship with fear, accepting that the most intense way to live is to be in synchronicity with the events crossing our path in life.

KEY TAKEAWAYS

1. Learning to live with uncertainty and complexity means accepting that we are part of a collective destiny that we can influence but cannot control. We should learn how to deal with unpredictability so that we do not shut down to create the false sensation of protection.

2. We have created a safety bubble, making us feel protected when conforming to the rules in place. This false sense of control misleads us by making us believe that the system protects us. It puts us in a passive position.

3. We can invite ourselves to see novelty and uncertainty as an opportunity to feel alive, connected to the elements, and in sync with others. All the unpredictable events we experience will take us on a new path, bringing us new pieces of life and unveiling the beauty of emergent realities.

4. While we have gained considerable brain time in the past centuries, the rise of digital tools is locking us down with a risky path of further disconnection from others and the world.

5. We are invited to shift from spending energy on fear to putting it in service to action. Acting is the best way to overcome fear. In taking an active approach, we can transform fears into powerful allies to shape the future we aspire to create for ourselves and the collective.

PRACTICAL REFLECTIONS

→ What are your biggest fears?

→ How do you approach your fears so that you can understand where they come from?

→ How do fears influence your life, and how can you use the energy they give you to act? Work on touching your jaguar.

→ How safe do you feel in your life? What makes you feel safe or unsafe?

→ How would you define 'stability'? How could you find your own stability in navigating uncertain situations?

→ How do you react in the face of challenging events? Reflect on how you shut down or open up in adversity.

→ What do you feel when learning about the world's state and potential risks the future could bring?

→ How do you translate crises into cracks, shedding light on new possibilities?

PART 3

LEADING FROM THE FUTURE

Seeing the world through new angles is eye-opening and transformational. It enables us to stand for what feels right to us and our collective future. It gives a new perspective to apprehend diverse realities and to determine what is critical to thrive.

The invitation is to leverage the insights gained through your self-introspection and the new pair of lenses you have started developing. The last part of the book is about aligning all the stars by combining your self-awareness, your place on the planet, and the unique contribution you can bring to the world. You are invited to sit with questions challenging your assumptions and setting the intention to birth a new part of yourself.

It will allow you to unlock your creativity and imagine possibilities to create the change you want to see in yourself and the world.

CHAPTER NINE

HOW DO YOU HOLD SPACE?

—

'It's a transformative experience to simply pause
instead of immediately filling up space.'
Pema Chödrön

E volving in the frenzy of society, it is easy to forget about ourselves. We get caught up in the pace of life and duties. My early calling to help others encouraged me to constantly make myself available to people who needed help. In doing so, I was taken away from the essential space I needed to reclaim to be available to myself. I started exploring what it meant to be available, reflecting on what it entailed and how to make it happen. While starting to reflect on it, I realised I could not stay on my own without being entertained by stimuli such as music, content or activities. I was addicted to doing things, refusing to stop and pause momentarily. The discomfort with myself was so disturbing that sitting alone without doing anything made me feel bored. At that time, I did not know how troubling that was for my existence. I was eating up my space with futile distractions, running away from myself.

My little revolution happened when a vision of circles appeared. I took a piece of paper and a pen and translated the picture I had in mind into a drawing. I drew a person at the page's centre and then a few circles around with arrows going outwards. I had put on paper the intention to move further away from the circles surrounding me to have more free space around myself.

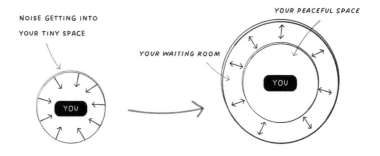

Figure 9: Making space for ourselves is needed to be at peace. Reclaiming this space is vital for you to thrive.

This visualisation was a metaphor expressing the need to take the vital space to be available to myself and refuse any form of intrusion from external people or events. Learning to be at peace with myself was to eliminate expectations, social pressures, and constant noise. The illustration followed me until today, constantly reminding me of the need to keep these circles of interaction at the proper distance to avoid being enslaved by time, space, or social expectations. It enabled me to choose what and who could stay in my inner circle—prioritising my attention and energy.

This approach offers an antidote to reject the expectations lying over our heads. The world order has taken citizens down, making us invisible and shutting down our own spaces of freedom. We slowly disappear, losing our space to care for, love, and look after ourselves. Ready to crash, we do our best to keep our heads above the water.

The reason is that we are part of a world designed for us, not by us. Codes and expectations mould our everyday behaviours, locking us into shrinking spaces. It is what we could call the 'gentrification of self'. Pressured by expectations, we have moved our gravity centre away from the core of our lives—losing balance in our existence. When codes and expectations take over too much space, we make ourselves small and invisible to survive the infernal pace of life. Boxing ourselves into a reality that revokes our access to thinking and being, we shut down, giving up on our wildest dreams and aspirations. This results in closing ourselves into boxes: house, office, car until the ultimate box that often comes up after death, the coffin. Is that really what we aspire our life to be?

The so-called modern world does not liberate us unless we wake up to create the new, saying 'yes' to what we genuinely want to be, feel, and experience. From being outsiders, we can become custodians of our future by repositioning our centre of gravity to take ownership of our lives.

HOLDING TIME AND SPACE FOR BEING

Social conventions weigh our lives down, cutting us off from the roots of our beings. In conforming, we obstruct our freedom to live within the space we deserve. We shut down our aspirations and desires to please the role we have been given without recognising ourselves in our choices and decisions. We obey the higher implied rules of society, never daring to reclaim our vital space to transition from a surviving to a thriving intention.

Our way of conforming to societal expectations is something we endure without question. We are subjugated by the 'what is' rather than letting ourselves imagine the 'what if' - inquiring about what tomorrow could be. This approach makes us lose our genuine desire for freedom, scaling down our ambitions to live a purposeful life through our values, intentions and aspirations. Today, conforming means fitting in with society and following the trend. On the contrary, doing things differently means taking the risk of excluding ourselves from the crowd. Peer pressure to stay on a conventional track discourages many of us and shuts down our imagination—making us afraid to reclaim our vital space.

Stuck in the traffic jams of our lives, we are not offered any exits to move away from the masses. We are surrounded by concentric circles, always eating up our space to put hurdles on our way to self-liberation. We are crushed into a daily shrinking space that asks us to play the contortionists into an always smaller space. Shaped by the crowd's beliefs, beliefs, judgements and our fear of missing out. We are collectively frozen. Until a majority embraces an authentic way of being, we will need personal courage to stand out from the herd. One after the other, there is the opportunity to form a new wave of change, liberating ourselves and inspiring others to follow as one collective.

The future invites us to a radically different mode of expression, where we can reclaim ownership of our lives by taking the space and time we urgently need. To move from enslavement, we must shift from a passive to an active posture with our space. We can take the lead in creating our own space and moving away from any barriers and struggles we impose on ourselves. We can learn how to set our boundaries where we used to set rules constraining us. It should not be about taking what we are given anymore but creating what we need.

Making space for ourselves starts with a deliberative choice of setting up our own rules for what is acceptable and what is not. As we would not accept anyone to have misplaced behaviour with us, why would we tolerate the mainstream to crash us down?

From this realisation, we can start resetting the rules we have taken for granted and realise that many scenarios are available. They are only waiting for us to imagine them and stick to their attributes so that we can live the life we aspire to live. By knowing who we are and our needs, we can clearly understand what space is necessary to express ourselves fully. It takes shape by practising to hold space, saying 'no' to societal pressures and 'yes' to live in harmony with our ideals.

Holding space for yourself is like taking a deep breath filled with peace to live a thriving existence. It furthers away the noise surrounding you and welcomes what can fuel your expansion. It can give you the freedom to choose your constraints and benefit from some duties you impose on yourself.

APPRECIATING TIME WITH SELF

We all have forms of great suffering within ourselves coming from events that have influenced our life and required us to bounce back. These layers of experiences, blending moments of pain and joy, blur our visibility of what is at the core of our lives. Within the deepest part of ourselves lies the treasure of self, where all our energy is waiting to be uncovered. To unpick these layers enables us to see life colourfully and find the diamond within ourselves. We need to learn how to be at ease with ourselves and face what triggers our fear, anxiety, and pain to live in peace.

The so-called 'liberation' concept supports the idea that as social beings, we constantly need to interact with groups and communities. While the social connection we develop with others and the world is critical, the first connection we are called to establish and nurture is with ourselves.

Despite this condition, many impulses encourage us to run away from spending time alone. From the distractions we receive, the need to be busy with others, to the interpretation of being alone as being excluded, few are the encouragements to be with ourselves. We often choose to move away from time with self, afraid of being ashamed, excluded, or perceived as deviant on top of being scared to reflect on ourselves. Our unconscious fear of facing our most profound truth discourages us from dedicating time to ourselves. Yet, one of the significant keys for us to shine into a full version of ourselves is to take the time and learn how to appreciate it. We have never been taught to be alone. Loneliness gives us the feeling that we are missing something, lacking love, attention, or the presence of others. It often puts us in a state of incompleteness and absence, leading to pain and sadness. But from this preconceived idea, we can embrace what being on our own can truly unleash within and for ourselves: aloneness.

On the contrary to loneliness, aloneness is when we feel fully present in the now, filled with fullness and aliveness, enjoying the simple fact of being in the moment and giving ourselves love. Aloneness helps us recognise that we are complete and enough. We must be on our own to experience a meditative process of self-attention. Learning to be quiet and still while being alone can be a significant step towards being in tune with aloneness. Gaining this ability makes us even more connected to our social relationships. Spending time alone can teach us how to value relationships, giving them even more importance and nurturing them with more attention.

To operate the shift from a painful to a peaceful state of mind being with ourselves, we need to nurture some essential principles. 'Presence is being': noticing anything that might make us uncomfortable and welcoming it as part of the experience. 'Coherence is alignment': being coherent with our authentic selves, following our guts and aspirations, whatever it takes. 'Abundance is infinity': moving from scarcity to abundance, being curious about anything we notice, being compassionate with ourselves and the world, and letting our creativity guide our experience. 'Patience is wiseness': being at ease with ourselves, the world and time, not being judgmental, defensive, or blameful while having these moments of quietness with self. 'Silence is a multitude of sounds': learning how to deal with silence can help us listen to what surrounds us and pay attention to all the interactions happening around us. 'Dancing is living': unleashing the true power of aloneness by dancing with life and being in rhythm with what comes our way.

BEING GENTLE WITH OURSELVES AND OTHERS

Our lives are paved by ups and downs that constantly influence our emotions, feelings, and attitudes. The path that takes us to quietude is never totally resolved. It represents a journey more than an ending point in space and time. While many are selling the idea that solutions exist to live the 'perfect life' and make the dream happen, the reality is much more complex. Contentment does not come from an end state, but from the awareness and sense of direction we embrace. It is something that makes us shine as we direct ourselves towards horizons that resonate with who we aspire to become.

To be gentle with ourselves comes first from being aware to develop what speaks to our heart. In exploring what makes you vibrate, self-care is essential not to burn your wings and keep on flying. It can become a driver for making space for a well-balanced process where you and others can receive what is needed. We all crave attention and love, which becomes imperative when expanding into new horizons. To care is to see, listen, and consider what is around and within us. Using our five senses, we can get to a higher level of consciousness where we can see, hear, smell, touch, and taste. All these senses can take us back on the right track so that we reconnect with ourselves, being gentle with what we are experiencing.

It is essential to pay attention and value anything that crosses our path, comes to our mind, or makes us feel. Seeing is to perceive in ourselves and others what goes through, being awake to empathise. In listening deeply, we can offer attention to ourselves and others. Let's be reminded that we have been given two ears and one mouth to prioritise deep listening before speaking our truth.

Key guiding principles can help us in our everyday lives. Miguel Ruiz's Four Agreements[40] depict four main drivers that are useful for advancing care for self and others. 'Being

---

[40] *The Four Agreements, Don Miguel Ruiz.*

impeccable with your word' is about taking responsibility for how we speak, choosing words carefully and with integrity not to hurt anyone when expressed. 'Don't take anything personally' takes you to the next level of confidence. Do not be hurt by anything that could be said to you, as comments reflect the perception and beliefs of a person projecting their reality into you. 'Don't make assumptions' is about avoiding unnecessary misunderstandings where interpretation misleads us, searching for clarity by asking questions rather than jumping to conclusions and imagining what others could think. Last but not least, 'Always do your best' entails welcoming the three first agreements and not restricting the energy we put into action, avoiding regretting anything or judging ourselves.

In following these agreements, you can reach the summits of making space and time for yourself. These are the ingredients to live with the necessary air to breathe your world, get to know yourself better and inspire others to follow your trail. Proceeding with this work opens up opportunities to relearn how to be in synchronicity with your inner world and what surrounds you. It also creates a healthy habit of living in flow with time, which implies using it more wisely. As Miguel Ruiz puts it, 'Every human is an artist. The dream of your life is to make beautiful art'.

KEY TAKEAWAYS

1. To care is to see, listen, and consider what is there around and within us using our five senses. It is to become aware to everything around us, perceiving the world as it is and as it evolves through us. It is part of recognising our interconnection with life and seeing ourselves as part of a broader system.

2. We are cornered by society's weight, pushing us towards the edge. It is as if we were given a role to serve rules we have not chosen. Pressured to deliver on societal standards, the model slowly eats up our space.

3. We urgently need to take time and space to look after ourselves. We must actively stand up for our boundaries, transitioning from being enslaved to supporting the system to serve our existence and the future of the collective.

4. To listen to our callings and needs is essential to nurture self-love, attention, and connection with the world. The practice of aloneness can help us be fully present, giving us the love we need and the space that can enable us to be at peace.

5. Silence plays a significant role in grounding and making us present. The musicality of silence can influence who we are and enable us to develop a greater sense of inner peace with ourselves and our relationship with the world.

PRACTICAL REFLECTIONS

→ What would it look like if you had to draw yourself and your place in the world?

→ Have you ever felt the need to go against the mainstream current to create your own way? If so, how did you proceed?

→ Do you have the courage to stand for your own space? How do you feel when doing it?

→ When did you last spend time alone without any technological or human distractions?

→ How do you feel when experiencing a moment of silence while alone? And with others? Think of your automatic response to silence and how you usually react in such situations.

→ Draw yourself with some circles representing the boundaries you want to set up for yourself so that you can protect your core. What would it look like?

→ Map out what goes against your values, will, and happiness. Using this mapping, draw or write down what a thriving future would look like for you, considering your needs and the ones of future generations. Set up strong intentions to make it a reality.

CHAPTER TEN

HOW DO YOU SOURCE CHANGE FROM WITHIN?

—

*'The future belongs to those who believe
in the beauty of their dreams.'*
Franklin D. Roosevelt

In a fast-moving world where uncertainty is at a peak, setting the scenes to explore our internal fire is essential to ground ourselves. Our life has taken us in specific directions, and the work we need to do is to look at our journey's patterns. I started my commitment to serving others early and naturally. I had the chance to do something that spoke to my heart but never asked myself what in my journey could inform the contribution I wanted to make to the world. I kept doing what I was already involved in without looking at the bigger picture of my early life patterns and how they could have influenced the place I was operating from. Being in service to others felt instinctive, but I needed to understand why I was so committed to giving it my complete dedication.

I have always been working in service to the most deprived. From vulnerable youth, women or individuals fleeing wars, I was investing time in doing my best to support them. This took me to several continents, collaborating with institutions, governments, local non-governmental organisations and businesses—always in service to people in need. I was doing it as it felt right and in complete alignment with the ideals of the world to which I wanted to contribute. But I never asked myself 'Why do you do what you do?'.

I remember this moment of enlightenment when I realised I needed to explore why I was doing all this. I was feeling so blessed to access all these incredible people bouncing back from hardship and thought it would be great to understand why I got in touch with them in the first place. Being here for them was not a professional duty but a natural calling. I was determined to make sense of it. I therefore decided to start the inquiry by mapping out my journey, understanding my inner motivations, and finding out how I was attracted to the field in which I was involved. I looked at all the events in my life, ranging from difficult experiences to moments of pure joy and clarity, spotting the crossroads of my existence. The picture became more evident when I understood that I was sourcing this devotion to others from my early childhood trauma. I responded to my lack of love, support, and attention by giving it to others at a stage in life when it was essential for them to bounce back. This work on my mission has become a game changer as I gained a much greater understanding of the role I wanted to play on the planet. It gave me a more precise direction of travel and life meaning. It was no longer about living passively but experiencing passionately.

Everything became crystal clear about how my unconscious took me to where I was while giving me a sense of where I wanted to travel in the future. Understanding and acknowledging where this life commitment was coming from helped me properly pay attention to the meaning of my existence, sourcing change from within. I was no longer randomly committed. I knew why I was so passionate about it, ready to give it all. This total devotion became evident when I understood how much I was willing to give up on myself to serve others.

This shift in understanding helped me transition from giving to others for the sake of it to bringing myself fully to the world realising my inner aspirations. This awakening activated all my senses, motivating me to shape my life around my north star of empowering others. It became my centre of gravity, providing me with the right pathway to keep growing. This revelation helped me make better decisions, become more resilient in adversity, and reconnect with my forgotten inner self. I had woken up. I knew the life I wanted to live, with a clear objective to aim for.

Inviting ourselves to make this work of sourcing the change we want to see in the world is complex. We have fallen into the trap of designing our lives in a way that makes us sleepy, feeling comfortable being numb when we are expected to follow informal rules. All supposedly to make our lives easy. It discourages us from taking the time to explore our wildest dreams, thinking that these dreams are unattainable. This view of the impossible has shut down our imagination of what could make us alive. We often give up on living a life centred around our deepest desires. We once again are encouraged to separate ourselves from the core of our presence on Earth, detaching from our inner drivers to live a meaningful existence. Too often afraid to be judged, constrained by time, or too unrealistic to awaken our aspirations and make them happen.

I remember a discussion with a friend about her dilemma between finding a sense of purpose and enjoying life. She did not have to make concessions between one or the other since embodying the change we want to see in our lives and the world is so much fun. It is a liberation giving us the means to make our lives more meaningful, sharing with the ones we love, expanding like never before, and celebrating life. It frees us from burdens, lightening us up to enjoy life at its best.

To quit our automatic pilot mode, we have to set strong intentions and reflect on the meaning we want to give to our lives. The quest for a purposeful life translates from passive participation to taking an active role in shaping the future we desire for ourselves and the world. No one should stop you from attaining your highest ideals. To query your mission is to listen to your inner gut and welcome life as an iterative process where nothing is settled, but a direction of travel can give you more depth. It is like embarking on an unexplored adventure. The path ahead cannot be written in advance but developed by reflecting on what has shaped you until today and what animates you daily. This path is something you will carve for yourself. It is a self-introspection activity that helps you to zoom out, getting the big picture vision of what your life has been until now, what drives it today, and what it could look like tomorrow.

Everyone speaks about purpose today with the misleading thought of focusing on the output rather than the process of aiming there. There is nothing wrong with not having a purpose. The real work is about sourcing the change from within to set up the sails heading towards the north star that speaks to your aspirations. Imagine your north star as this star up there in the sky, shining to inform your direction of travel. Day and night, it gives you a compass to move closer to your aspirations. This precious guide informs your journey, helping you build the right experiences to get closer to your highest ideals. Whatever happens in your life, your north star will be your best ally to live harmoniously with the world you aspire to birth for yourself and generations to come.

In taking the step to explore your role on Earth, you will be able to transition from time to energy. You will discover that when you gain clarity on your intentions, you can reorganise your life with clear aspirations, fuelling your soul, heart, and mind. Being in quest of your mission is like looking at your balance in life, focusing on finding your equilibrium point where you can believe in the beauty of your dreams and get closer to them daily.

REFLECTING ON LEARNINGS

A north star does not fall out of the sky. While many might complain about how their day-to-day looks, it is our duty not to point fingers at the situation but to wake up to ensure we put in the necessary energy to advance our vision. The perceived gloominess of our lives reflects how we deal with them, giving up on investing the right amount of energy and attention. The world we perceive and experience reflects the energy we give to it. As Rainer Maria Rilke wrote, 'If your daily life seems poor, do not blame it; blame yourself, tell yourself that you are not poet enough to call forth its riches'.

We all have golden insights from experiences waiting for us to leverage them into fantastic drivers of meaning in our lives. We must accept being in charge of putting them together to write our story, taking ownership of our existence, and being accountable for how we evolve. Our lives constantly expand, linking yesterday with today and today with tomorrow. We evolve as we breathe, listen, and feel. Imagine a never-ending staircase where each step would represent a life event. Our journeys are about climbing it up, one experience at a time. We build on our previous knowledge from each event, creating a more substantial base to welcome the next experience.

While we have convinced ourselves that we can only fail or win, the reality is much more subtle. All lived experiences provide us with a precious takeaway. There is no such thing as victory or defeat in life events. We always gain input that takes us to the next stage of ourselves. Accepting and welcoming such insights can support our personal development, and expand our knowledge. Looking back at events that have represented significant changes in our journey can help us better understand our life itinerary.

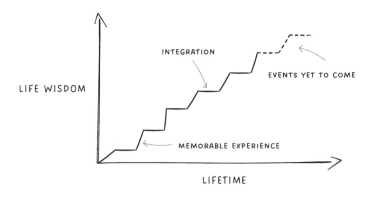

Figure 10: The staircase of life is composed of successive events transforming our existence. Each event is an opportunity to gain new perspectives and climb the stairs of life.

Knowing ourselves better through introspection, we can tap into a wealth of knowledge we have yet to uncover properly. Many events have influenced our lives, from a challenge in childhood, a beautiful memory as a teenager, a unique friendship bringing joy, a dark time of deep uncertainty, a health issue, a feeling of fulfilment, or a new experience. All of them are incredibly valuable in informing how we became who we are and how we can aspire to become the next version of ourselves.

This reflection can help us depict how doubts and clarity have emerged from such events guiding our journey until now. It enables us to understand better how situations have repeated over time, discovering patterns of existence with settings that trigger our specific reactions. The mapping of past experiences invites us to undress our protected selves better and let the diverse layers of influence we have collected emerge. It helps us demystify our evolving identity, understanding the many elements lying under the way we see ourselves and are seen by others. From this process, we can understand that we are made up of multiple chapters.

The granular exploration of experiences goes hand in hand with understanding our needs and what can trigger some of our emotions. This is an incredible opportunity to combine all our experiences to harvest knowledge on what we have endured until now, getting to know ourselves better and making wiser choices for the future we are co-creating.

INQUIRING ABOUT THE JOURNEY AHEAD

The mainstream way of thinking rewards us for quick answers to problems that arise. The gain has become driven by short-term so-called solutions that are, in reality, only plasters to more profound reflections that need time to be fruitful. The same is true with the meaning we can give to our lives. To truly source change from within is to accept that life is not a ticket to happiness but a journey to experience.

The process includes many exciting questions that will take us one step closer to the answer. Wisdom comes from endless back-and-forth experiences of emotions, decisions, and interactions. To help this inquiry come to life, we need to get rid of our expectations to find solutions, welcome any thought that arises, and take it as a clue for us to move forward. The exercise of inquiring about what your future could bring is driven by who you are, what you like, what you could become good at, what the world looks like, and how these diverse forces can come together to help you find the right path.

To do so, it is key to look at what matters for you, reflecting on what speaks to your heart at this very moment in your life and how its importance has developed over time. What do you feel is unfair in the world today? Where is the need for justice? Whether you care about regenerating local forests, protecting endangered species, supporting disabled youth, providing opportunities to single mothers, educating children in need, or enabling community cohesion, there is a role waiting for you. There are unlimited possibilities for you to do good for yourself and others. From this, you can reflect on what you enjoy doing, looking at previous experiences that have filled you with joy when being involved in specific tasks, with particular objectives, and with the presence of certain people. Let's say you love to support people to advance an objective collectively, enjoy being creative in your day-to-day or appreciate having supportive people around you. This will enlighten your understanding of what you are good at doing and where you are interested in developing your skills and abilities so that you can put them in service to a greater cause. Whether you excel at bringing people together, communicating and inspiring or creating, there is a space for you to unleash your full potential.

Because you live in a relationship with the world and are not an isolated being, it is essential to reflect on how the world looks today and where the most urgent needs are for building a prosperous future for all. Look at today's society and reflect on what needs your time and attention. From the climate crisis to various social issues, plenty of challenges are waiting for you to engage. In combining your aspirations with the bigger needs of the world, you can explore a pathway to sourcing change from within, putting yourself in service to something bigger.

Sourcing change from within involves deep diving into who you are, what you genuinely believe in, and what you would like the world to look like. It can support you so that you can fully understand what change you want to see happening. It is a journey of putting yourself in motion to make a unique contribution to the world that speaks to your heart and serves the many. What role could be yours on the planet?

It is an invitation that goes hand in hand with the idea that everything not given in life is wasted, and so is our energy when it is not given to a more significant cause. It encourages us to find where we want to give, ensuring we use our potential wisely by being in service to what Simon

Sinek calls a 'just cause'[41]. A just cause is something we stand for and believe that brings hope to create a better future. It is inclusive to invite anyone who wants to rally to be invited to it, and service-oriented to support anyone who needs help. It should also be resilient so it can endure changes such as political, technological, cultural, or climate crises. Last but not least, a just cause should be idealistic and bold, with an ambition high enough to bring real change to the world. To start this inquiry is to explore how we would like to contribute to the world in a fulfilling way for us, the collective, and the living world we belong to.

The beauty of inquiring about our north star is to gain insights from setting up a context that will host our day-to-day activities and actions. Every step of our life walking towards the direction of its meaning can represent an empowering move that can be celebrated and become an encouragement to keep walking for the just cause we have set for ourselves. It can inform our decisions not to rely on short-term wins but rather on the big-picture intentions of the meaning we want to give to our lives. From finite goals of achieving something, we instead use every step of the journey as a springboard to the next one. This takes us back to the metaphor of the staircase of life, making one experience at a time to build the ramp towards our north star. Aiming for the star, we are building our ladder of life.

---

[41] *The infinite game, Simon Sinek.*

SETTING OURSELVES IN MOTION

Understanding where the change is within ourselves is a milestone that helps us take a significant step towards understanding what our unique contribution can be. From acknowledging it, we are invited to operate the shift, putting this vision at the core of our existence. This is a practice where we let ourselves explore the true meaning of the change we want to see in the world and how it can manifest. Once again, it is about the journey and not the goal itself. It is fine not to have a perfect articulation of what change you want to make as long as you gain a sense of direction about where you want to head and find resonance with life on Earth. It is to find meaning in our lives to be fulfilled with continuous energy towards the future we are carving for ourselves.

The path is transformational, transitioning from various stages of awareness, and taking us a step further. It allows us to find coherence with ourselves by welcoming these phases as a constant evolution of our personalities. This exercise is proactive with an engagement to be in right relationship with what surrounds us, being aware of our past and the legacy we carry from previous generations. While reflecting on it, we need to acknowledge the concept of Ubuntu[42], recognising that 'I am because we are' and seeing how the change we want to make in the world will have

---

[42] *Ubuntu is a term originating from southern Africa and the Nguni peoples meaning 'humanity'. It is commonly translated as 'I am because we are'.*

ripple effects on the whole system surrounding us, including people and the planet. This approach will be fueled by our work leveraging our self-introspection insights to get to know ourselves better and dedicate time to what feels right. In doing so, we will also inspire others around us to help peers to 'being more' rather than 'having more'.

Aiming for your north star, you will be taken on an unexplored path, welcoming novelty and appreciating any emotion that can emerge from the adventure. Life will become much more meaningful and fun as you enter this new phase of taking charge. This fluid experience will keep energising your path, adding new experiences and informing you of your direction. By having the courage to stand up for your ideals, you will open up a new field of possibilities transforming your relationship with time, uncertainty, and life itself. You will enable a profound change that will help you shift from a time perspective to a flow of energy sourced from your highest aspirations.

As you unveil your deepest desires, you will start seeing the potential of what the future holds. You will be able to find clarity, transforming what used to be scarce time into an unlimited flow of energy, always taking you closer to where you want to head. Serving a cause beyond your existence can empower you to shape the future with responsibility and care. It will not be about pulling anymore. The stars will finally align, allowing you to flow. Time will not be a limitation anymore, as your focus will be on what deeply matters to you.

KEY TAKEAWAYS

1. Exploring our north star is not to search for a solution but a broader sense of meaning in our lives. It is to find a centre of gravity that can help us move towards something bigger than us. It is an awakening of the soul, unveiling the inner treasure sleeping within ourselves.

2. Every life experience is a pocket of wisdom we carry that can help us get to know ourselves better. There is no such thing as failure or victory. Any experience represents an opportunity to get closer to our north star.

3. The most important is not the outcome but the journey. Inquiry is a journey to experience rather than a ticket to happiness. The wisdom we develop is an endless process of back-and-forth, where the essential is to go after the direction that speaks to our heart. Make it beat.

4. To find meaning in our lives, we are called to shift from having more to being more. We must eliminate societal expectations and consumption models to welcome ourselves with purity. We can discover how little we need to be fulfilled and happy by fully being.

5. To take ownership of your life is to become responsible for the future you are carving for yourself and the collective. It is an invitation to give energy to what you believe in. Life mirrors our attitudes and approaches.

PRACTICAL REFLECTIONS

→ Why do you do what you do in life? From your job to your decisions, inquire about the meaning of the important roles you play in life.

→ What are some of the memorable experiences that influenced the path of your life?

→ In which situations do you feel a sense of completeness?

→ What situations brought you joy and contentment?

→ What do you like and enjoy doing?

→ What are the main strengths and abilities you can put in service to a greater cause?

→ What are the most critical societal issues that we, citizens, need to work on?

→ What would be the ideal contribution(s) you could make to the world?

→ Imagine you could do anything that aligns with who you are and what you want to become. What would it be?

CHAPTER ELEVEN

HOW DO YOU STAND FOR YOUR IDEALS?

—

'The ultimate measure of a man is not where he stands in moments of comfort and convenience, but where he stands at times of challenge and controversy.'
Martin Luther King

To be ourselves is to lead the life we desire and aspire to create. One knows how difficult it can be to find our place in the world so it is to show up to the world, bringing our whole selves to life. When starting my journey of inner worlds, I often felt I needed to be more confident about how others could react to my choices and convictions. From being part of the mass to standing up when things did not feel in alignment with the person I was, I have experienced firsthand the shift of others' perceptions. To openly criticise the establishment and live a parallel existence proposing something new was not easily accepted and understood. Despite the many challenges, I decided to stand for what I believed in encouraging dialogue to trigger the thinking of others.

I knew I was not holding the truth but experimenting with something different, often perceived as unconventional. From my meandering in diverse countries to the choice of not being constrained by time, some of my closest peers were worried, while new encounters were sometimes scared off. Others were supportive and often inspired by the benefits of such choices.

I experienced being in the spotlight for judgement and criticism by others. I accepted it as it was essential to me to stand for my values and beliefs. It made me lose people with whom I certainly did not have enough of a connection for them to welcome my convictions. In the meantime, I became much closer to people with whom I sometimes had divergent views but were fully open to growing by our differences. I then realised that making these active stands on what was guiding my life and decisions was a fantastic driver for others to source inspiration in doing the same. It made my existence much more fluid and helped me align with my north star.

From implementing a 'less but better' lifestyle to initiating more conscious practices, I saw how people surrounding me adopted some forms of similar patterns. It encouraged them to open up space for unconventional novelty to emerge. This made me understand that being true to ourselves and others is the best way to move collectively to greater levels of ethics and ideals. Until you create the breach for yourself and others, a great dose of courage is required, as you are likely stuck in the static reality of your peers.

The multiple conversations along my journey have taught me the importance of healthy debates and disagreements. Many challenging conversations helped me question my views, reaffirming some core values while encouraging me to evolve in my way of thinking. Learning to disagree helps us see our opinions through various angles while welcoming stronger convictions of why we believe this way. In accepting that my values and beliefs were evolving and personal, I learned that projecting them into others was not the way to go. I welcomed differences as the opportunity to grow together, sharing various perspectives to help one another progress towards closer ideals. This is why we need to do the exercise to communicate our thoughts and beliefs to others. This is a way to enrich our perspectives by also welcoming differences. We are encouraged to explore our guiding principles and relate them to our internal structure to make decisions informed by our values, convictions, and beliefs.

Through the way we live, we constantly make choices that reflect who we are at this moment in time, uncovering some of our personality traits to others. It can therefore seem complicated in a setting where we feel judged and criticised for any step we take. It requires us to learn how to stand for what feels right, be ready to be challenged and realise how to help others gain access to new perspectives.

The power of the single story is so strong that we often feel overwhelmed by society's pressure. From the way we dress, speak, eat, identify, entertain ourselves, or feel connected to others, the hidden rules of our lives will always aim to put our differences down. It is like invisible hands trying to put us back on the right track from the mainstream perspective. Imagine swimming against the flow. This is how our lives can look when we stand for something unique that differs from the most common perspectives.

The difference we can make is when we truly believe in our path, gaining the energy to keep moving forward whatever others are thinking and constantly communicating our vision without fear of reprisal or disagreement. We can take our independence of view and opinion to advance what feels right, following our guts and instincts. This is the reason why finding a tribe of people supporting you on the journey can become an excellent enabler to take the step of standing for what feels right.

From family to friends, colleagues, and even people we cross paths with, all send signals influencing our journeys in life. How they look at, speak to, and think about us can shake our way of being, questioning our choices or opinions. While this process can reveal being healthy for not camping on our positions forever, we need to anchor ourselves into what we genuinely believe to avoid losing track of what matters to us. This anchor comes from exercises of self-introspection, growing ourselves through encounters and experiences. Combining every piece of life allows us to step for our identity and not be afraid to show up as we speak our truth. Whether people like it or not, we are moving as we intend.

There is tremendous power in being true to yourself to become an example for the many who have yet to stand up for themselves. In communicating who you are and what you believe in, you can shed light on the importance of aligning your aspirations with how you advance your life. You can lead by example, putting your words into action and living a life that aligns with your highest ideals. In the meantime, developing a form of openness towards critics and new experiences is essential to inform your opinions and keep transforming yourself with the latest events and encounters, inspiring you to grow. Your way of thinking will be highly beneficial as it evolves with time as you gain perspectives and collect wisdom.

KNOWING YOUR VALUES

To know your values, you first need to know yourself. As we explored in the self-introspection part of this book, having a sense of identity is crucial to getting to know what matters to you. As you initiate this work of getting to know yourself better, values can emerge, becoming the lived perspective of the life you envision. To get to know your values is all about looking at what guiding principles you want to become the driving force of your life. Values are guiding principles that inform and influence your decisions and behaviours, giving you a sense of what feels right. They shape your beliefs, attitudes, and actions so that you can evolve and move in the right direction.

In a world driven by monetary value, we have been diverted from our core human values, playing the game of competition to access positions of domination. We have been encouraged to give up on our values to conform to the crowd. This has led us to detach ourselves from grounding values and ethics of respect, dignity, and reciprocity with a new mindset responding to our fears. A mindset which makes us more selfish and competitive with others. This homogenisation has highly influenced our personalities, moving from an alignment of values with who we are to a whole new world where we have drifted away from our core. Values can be personal but also profoundly linked to specific cultures, becoming a universally held standard by a group of people. This standardisation has oppressed many of us from bringing ourselves into the world, becoming constrained to fit our surroundings.

When not aware of our values, our decisions are often influenced by the expectations of people around us. Instead of adopting a values-driven approach to inform our choices, we are trying to please others. If you reflect on how you make decisions, you may realise that you have done so much under the influence of what society calls you to do or the implicit messages you have received from people around you. To please others against our core values should not be the way as it distracts us from our life course. Our time is too valuable to be wasted on making decisions that undermine our well-being and, therefore, our attitudes towards others.

Reclaiming our independence is a much-needed step towards understanding and applying what can guide us to the future we want to create for ourselves. Indeed, understanding our values is a significant milestone before applying them to live following our direction of travel. It gives us a guide rail to make better and easier decisions, choosing what is suitable for us rather than what is expected of us.

Following Gandhi's words, 'Your beliefs become your thoughts, your thoughts become your words, your words become your actions, your actions become your habits, your habits become your values, your values become your destiny'. Having a clear understanding of your values is crucial for making decisions aligned with your direction of travel, prioritising your desires, and living in accordance with your genuine self.

BEING GUIDED BY BELIEFS

Our truths are built upon our lived experiences through what we have seen, heard, and witnessed. We create our truth from the mosaic of stimuli we have received and accumulated—often biased by our mono-lens perspective. This truth of ours then builds up our convictions, shaping our opinions. While our world is increasingly connected, local realities are very different, creating diverse beliefs depending on where we live, who we spend time with, and how we inform ourselves. Our truths are unique and, in so many ways, imperfect. Still, they are worth communicating and sharing with others to enrich the healthy debate of convictions.

When we believe, we are putting our energy into defending the idea that truth lies there. Cultural, religious or personal lived experiences can influence our beliefs. They can vary from deep convictions, where we would not give up on a perspective, to tentative beliefs, where we still make up our minds about a particular opinion. This is a constant iterative process where we go back and forth with our tentative beliefs, giving up on some or deepening others for them to become strong convictions. They can change over time as we gain new information or experience novelty.

To believe can be to our advantage as it gives us a strong understanding of the reality we want to create, enabling us to have a clear path towards supporting what feels right. It is a big part of our identities that helps us define ourselves amid conflicts or challenges. It represents a solid base enabling us to stand for what we are convinced of. This liberates us from the pressure of feeling lost, giving us a sense of direction. To believe is to source energy from what matters to us and how we can defend our point of view. Anyone should find their beliefs to be on track to achieve their ideals.

Nevertheless, in an era of disinformation, fake news, and conspiracy theories, many citizens have lost their capacity to filter information and can adopt beliefs based on rumours or false information. It is a critical danger for the evolution of humanity as it makes room for manipulating parts of the population using their existing preconceptions to create shared beliefs based upon fake information. This is why it is essential to confront ourselves with multiple perspectives outside our peer groups and use various sources of information that challenge our truth.

To believe is also to belong, as we are pulled towards others who think alike. While this can create echo chambers of individuals thinking in bubbles, it can also create a strong momentum for us to find allies willing to share the journey with us—leading to positive or negative outcomes. We have seen, for instance, the rise of a climate movement with individuals worldwide sharing their worries for the future of humanity, uniting forces through public demonstrations, civil disobedience, or community projects. In the meantime, we see the growing threat of political discourses to divide citizens based on their gender, race, or education. It shows how belief can turn into a spiral of belonging for the better or the worse.

HAVING THE COURAGE TO REVISIT

We all feel safe camping in our positions, but it is often good to look away from our common preconceptions and observe what is happening outside our circles of influence. Our values and beliefs are essential to moving forward, but as we evolve, they can also become outdated or imperfectly adapted to the person we aspire to become. This adjustment is part of our existence, giving it space to happen without fearing to ask ourselves questions about how to get closer to our next set of beliefs and values. It invites us to welcome once again vulnerability, having the courage to face interrogations and rethink our way of seeing the world and making decisions.

The complexity in this comes from society's fixed mindset, which does not encourage revisiting our beliefs and values. Instead, we often follow the ones shaped by our narrow reality of life experiences. Imagine using a device with the same settings without considering personalising it. Most of us do this by unconsciously following standards without questioning what we stand for. It requires courage and critical thinking to explore how they have come to life and if they are still fit for purpose.

It is a great help to think of the negative and false beliefs we can have about who we are, as they limit our capacity to expand. These limiting beliefs often relate to the idea we make of ourselves as not worthy of love, care, or affection. In believing so, we think negatively about ourselves and create barriers to our range of experiences, limiting ourselves from interactions with the world. It often comes from our subconscious and becomes beliefs that impact our existence, propagating preconceived ideas. We need to question them to understand where they come from and how to get rid of them.

Challenging our beliefs is in our best interest to reflect and rethink. It is essential to leave room for discussion and debate when revisiting so we can be open to constantly evolving. It is like welcoming a fresh breath into the world, reimagining what could be our new drivers for a fulfilled existence. It is hard for us to do so as we build our identities upon beliefs and values which are inextricably linked to emotions. These emotions can provoke discomfort and challenge what we used to take for granted.

The best way to let yourself revisit your beliefs and values is to listen to who you are. Your subconscious always acts on your behalf making you unable to notice how you think anymore. Identify the automated processes in your mind by asking yourself questions about what comes to mind. In giving space to see how you think, you can explore how your beliefs have taken over your mind and learn how to apprehend, question and revisit them. This process will then inform the complementary experience you need to pursue, expanding your understanding of life and becoming a guide towards the future you want to create for yourself. If you dare to revisit your values and beliefs, you will also stand for what feels right.

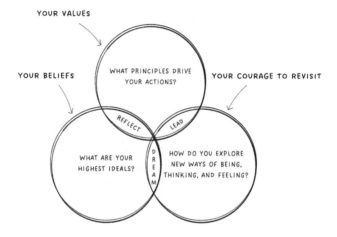

Figure 11: The exploration of our beliefs and values is a never-ending inquiry. There is so much we can gain from asking ourselves what motivates our actions, what we envision, and how we can explore how to revisit what we took for granted.

KEY TAKEAWAYS

1. Bringing ourselves to the world and communicating who we are can be scary. We have developed many layers of shame from the pressure felt by the judgement of others. To stand with our differences is to liberate ourselves from an immense weight realigning with the person we are proud of being.

2. We can use our differences to trigger unexplored areas of our existence, opening up new ways of thinking. In creating healthy debates with others to discuss our opinions, values, and beliefs, we can move away from the single-perspective story.

3. Society has defined value as an economic term focusing on gain, possession and power. To bring humanity back to human values, we need to stand for what feels right instead of what is expected of us. Our values guide our direction of travel.

4. Our beliefs give us a robust understanding of the reality we want to create. They provide clues about the path we want to walk to make our convictions a reality. To believe is to source energy from what matters.

5. Nothing is settled in life, nor are our values and beliefs. From rigid thinking, we need to open up ourselves to challenge our views and give space to others to share theirs.

PRACTICAL REFLECTIONS

→ How aligned do you feel with the person you are inside and how you show up to the world?

→ What does integrity mean for you?

→ What keeps you away from bringing your whole self to the world?

→ What values are driving your behaviours, and how do you express them in your day-to-day life?

→ What beliefs animate your life, and how do you follow them?

→ How could you share and listen to others' convictions even when different from yours?

→ What can stimulate your inquiries so that you discover unexplored paths that inform your way of believing and standing in the world?

→ How do you challenge your beliefs and values so that you can explore new horizons of thinking?

CHAPTER TWELVE

HOW CAN YOU LEAD POSITIVE CHANGE?

—

'Every great dream begins with a dreamer. Always remember,
you have within you the strength, the patience, and the
passion to reach for the stars to change the world.'
Harriet Tubmanure

To build a radically new future, we need to be leading differently. We need to reinvent our societies with disruptive novelty that challenges the status quo. The great news is that alternative ways emerge from the current landscape, suggesting a new path for ourselves and the world. As we grapple with multilayered crises, we cannot sit back and resign from trying something new. We know how needed our awakening is to transform our obsolete world. While there are already millions of people around the globe creating something new for themselves and their communities, no one will come for us to lead positive change until we fully take ownership of it and shape the new. The key lies in activating our internal fire to plant the seeds of what tomorrow could be.

I saw how this fire could become a driver to imagine the possibilities of a different future. I met hundreds of changemakers, creating something new for themselves and positively impacting the world. From escaping the poverty trap to supporting the education of their community, empowering others to lead change, or recovering from depression, all the people I encountered have been a magical source of inspiration when it comes to their ability to spring from a challenging state to the authentic version of themselves. In finding their true selves, they started shining to the world, contaminating others to become more conscious and lead positive change.

I observed the same light in these citizens, sparkling from their life lessons and the clarity they have gained through their inquiries. Passion animates their heads, hearts, and hands, making the new. Their thinking goes beyond the existing—sourcing from the contributions of others, filling them up with ideas, energy, and perspectives that can support them in creating a better version of themselves. I experienced the power of constellations by being immersed in various realities and reunited with diverse people. It helped me gain insights, activating my head to think about what tomorrow could bring, my heart to feel the world as it could become, and my hands to build a new kind of dream alongside others.

I realised how leading from a place of connection could change the richness of our interactions. Giving space to others to be rather than pretend can revolutionise their way of showing up and coming together. To go with humility about not knowing when approaching a question has revealed being a game-changer in how I built coalitions of people and facilitated conversations to co-create the yet-to-exist experimentation.

We are all artists of our lives and common future. While the aesthetic of the beautiful has been colonised with the standardisation of capitalism, we should allow ourselves the opportunity to make beautiful art again. Inviting ourselves to try new experiences to see what the world could be and design something that can provide humanity with a long-term perspective of hope, joy, and fulfilment. To become the changemakers of tomorrow, we have to reset our way of being, thinking, and imagining the future we fear to desire. Beyond its direct intrusion into our lifestyle, the world order takes us collectively into a very uncertain future where risks grow exponentially. If we do not change the system in which we operate, we are heading for disaster.

From how we see value to our attitude towards others and the living world, we are running after the wrong objective. All this is slowly killing our ability to be in right relationship with life. It can no longer be the way. We have to wake up from this numb existence to spring into the authentic version of ourselves, supporting the co-creation of a thriving and equitable tomorrow. It is time for you to regain influence over your life, question yourself about what you want, and create something magical that honours life on Earth. What are your deepest desires?

The wave of change is here. You are part of it. Whatever stage in life and the meaning you want to give to it, you are not just the future but also the here and now. This power you have in your hands is waiting to be used in service to a greater future. What if you could lend your most extraordinary talents to a cause you care about?

You might not be able to solve a problem alone, but it is even truer that we cannot solve it without you. This is a collective endeavour, and we need to succeed as a team. It is our collective future that is at stake. We could choose to continue the course of our lives as they are today, hiding behind our duties, the supposed lack of time, and the complexity of changing the system. But our times are too urgent. We are compelled to join the movement of awakened citizens, taking our lives into our own hands and co-creating a future that makes us live with the will to make the dream happen.

For this shift to operate in practice, we need to bring the best of ourselves alongside others to reinvent the codes, making the old system obsolete. We need to radically reinvent our way of teaming up with others, moving away from competition to welcome open attitudes. Adopt an approach where our differences become a strength to propose a coherent version of society that reflects the needs of the many over the few. It is our opportunity to move away from scarcity to welcome abundance, where everyone can get their fair share of the efforts made to advance the world as one.

Multiple futures are within reach. Our role is to make the one we want to see become a reality. In the future we can create, many will emerge to match local realities moving away from globalisation to welcome glocalisation[43]. Groups of individuals will continue to be formed and come together to create something fit for the needs of their communities. In taking the chance to create something unique, you will be able to craft something special resonating with your values, expressing yourself, and serving the collective. The multi-facets of this work are where the beauty lies. It is our chance to give space for creativity and become the driving force of a future that aligns with the world we desire. With this enriched vision of tomorrow, we are ready to enter a new era of possibilities. Creativity is all of us.

LEADING THE NEW WAY FORWARD

As we enter a cornerstone of human history, our generation's challenge is to reconnect ourselves to one another and the living world. The current form of leadership ruling our society is outdated. It still uses the old software of what power used to be. This cannot be the way if we want individuals to flourish and thrive in a world that needs reinventing. To co-create a better future, we need a new direction where citizens are leading from the future. Enlightened individuals who understand the importance of

---

[43] *Glocalisation is a combination of the words 'globalisation' and 'localisation'. It expresses the idea of using our global knowledge and interconnection applied to the needs at a local level.*

belonging and interdependence can unveil this new leadership. All of us are leaders of our own lives. We also influence many around us through our way of being. It calls on us to recognise our relationship to the living world and accept our interconnectedness, taking responsibility for it.

This new form of leadership allows us to renew our symbiotic relationship with the living world. Refusing to keep on with the status quo of dominance, we deserve to find our true way of belonging in a world that speaks to who we are and what we believe in. Bio Leadership opens the way forward by proposing an alternative story that can unleash the power of relationships through compassion, kindness, and reciprocity. It offers a radical alternative to heal the separation mindset and the paradigm of lack, extraction and exploitation by replacing it with a new model based on connection and thriving. Such a story could inspire the much-needed impetus for restoring our planet and unleashing our fullest human potential.

Moving from 'I' to 'We' offers the possibility of conceptualising a new paradigm deeply connected to the Earth and our fellow citizens. It delivers on the aspiration to shape a new paradigm where harmony can empower individuals to lead their way in favour of a just and equitable future. The key traits of Bio Leadership are sourced from natural cycles and relationships that have existed for centuries on our planet. Seven main guiding principles drive this new way of leading: resilience, radical collaboration, empowered potential, nurtured connections, harmony, wholeness, and space.

Resilience is all about taking advantage of our journeys, and honouring struggles in life to bounce back to a better version of ourselves. It is about letting go of the so-called 'failures', seeing them as opportunities to grow our inner world and share our wisdom with others. Let's not ignore our challenges but welcome their memory to build a better version of ourselves. It adds to the importance of radical collaboration, helping us move away from domination and the furious competition of our societies to being in symbiosis with others, valuing diversity. It is about recognising that our individualistic mindset will not take us as far as coming together to reflect and get things done. It is no longer about seeing others as a potential danger to ourselves but rather seeing their participation as an asset for the collective.

We all face limits and boundaries, but when empowered, we can find the keys to getting to know ourselves and lead with our convictions. In the value we give to others, we must empower everyone's potential, helping one another to express the best version of ourselves. This support directly connects to the importance of nurtured connections. We belong to a broader system than ourselves. This idea invites us to recognise the relationships that have made us who we are—acknowledging, valuing, and celebrating our interdependence. It comes back to being aware and grateful for all our ties to the world that set us in motion and can help us resonate.

To resonate is to find harmony, balance, and equilibrium in a shaky world. In line with the Yin and Yang theory, harmony invites us to welcome opposite forces with the emergence that arises from diverse people, places, and insights. Our role is to weigh our decisions, considering how diverse thinking, cultures, and minds can come together for one common goal.

Wholeness embeds the importance of seeing people and the world as a combination of multiple traits and attributes. We must recognise the uniqueness of each place, person, and situation, letting them express their entire identity and personality. We can learn from anyone or any situation and, therefore, should provide space for the emergence of different perspectives. This closes the loop of Bio Leadership principles, which emphasise the importance of holding space to enable trust so that we and others feel safe while exploring our identities. Learning and experimenting always require special attention and the confidence to go off the beaten tracks. Holding space for someone is like giving an extra chance to ourselves and others to open a new chapter of our stories.

These principles are the driving force for you to inspire change within yourself and your community. In leading by example, you can spearhead a new movement of conscious leaders committed to supporting the call for life. To implement the principles, one should have done the work of knowing oneself, facing the demons of the past and understanding its identity. These principles are potent counsellors and an excellent ally for moving away from disconnection and finding resonance again with the living world.

UNLEASHING THE POWER OF INQUIRY

The obsolete approach is about making shallow work on problems without truly tackling root causes. On the other hand, the world we are ready to unveil makes us at peace with questions being the drivers of our existence. Being humble enough not to pretend to know can help us transition from the old mindset to welcome the new. The current model has made us believe that quick solutions will be found for every challenge we face. Nevertheless, every challenge is an opportunity to ask ourselves new questions, opening our senses to inquire about the possibilities. We have been tweaked to think through logical thinking, which influences our attitude towards so-called challenges and uncertainty. It is time to feel the world vibrating under our feet.

We must craft something radically different to create what tomorrow could look like. A new story is at reach, translating the power of inquiries to perform our common path towards aligning our heads, hearts, and hands to liberate our global potential. Accepting not knowing and welcoming any new experience is teaching us the way.

Our heads can help us get to the level of strategic thinking, putting ideas into action using our capacity to reflect. Our hearts can inform us about our internal callings following our emotions, passion, and commitment to deliver something unique. Our hands are then at our disposal to live practical experiences and bring all the emotions and thinking into something practical that can transform ourselves and the world around us. By becoming aware of our diverse sources of inspiration and action, we can combine their power into making powerful inquiries where questions drive the adventure of imagining the future.

The beauty of inquiring about the future is to do it together, bringing ourselves to the collective. We can source more energy by welcoming our interconnection to one another and the world, finding allies to co-create. In asking ourselves and others questions, we can take advantage of multiple opinions and ideas, making the experience a wonderful adventure. We are called to welcome diversity to debate, suggest, and co-create together—fostering diversity, equity, and inclusion. As Vernā Myers[44] puts it, 'diversity' means everyone gets invited to the party, 'equity' that everyone can contribute to the playlist and 'inclusion' that everyone can dance. In being ourselves as part of a collective, we can dance together, creating our unique choreography of what the world could look like, making it joyful, collaborative, and hopeful.

It is where the collective can truly bring its value in service to the future we want to unfold. In coming together, we can liberate a new energy powering diverse ideas that can radically disrupt the status quo. We are called to avoid the mistakes of the way society has been built, which has led to a single perspective of the Western world. We are invited to learn how to listen to others, giving space for multiple perspectives while sharing our views concisely to make our

---

[44] *Vernā Myers is an American diversity consultant, author, speaker, lawyer, and corporate executive.*

unique contribution to co-shaping tomorrow. Let us welcome contradictory points of view and mindsets to design solutions to complex problems we face. This is our duty and our extraordinary opportunity to liberate our collective potential for a thriving society serving the interests of all.

IMAGINING A THRIVING FUTURE

Our current system does not satisfy human needs. It unnecessarily wastes our precious time, resources, and attention. The great news is that the system is cracking from all parts. The heaviness and establishment of the old make it survive, but society, as it exists, cannot keep going like this. Our collective boat is sinking, with pieces breaking apart and water starting to flow in. While the ones sustaining the old system are trying to fill the broken parts, the wave of change can flip the boat, making it sink for us to build a new human raft, taking us towards new desirable futures.

The cracks in the system are leaving space for the new to emerge, providing us with some rays of light and encouraging us to find our way through the hope of reinventing the world we want to live in. To get rid of the old and welcome the new, we need to liberate our imagination to craft something we have not yet imagined possible. Against relentless productivity, we can praise a sufficient society where we can have enough to live well.

The new could shift to use-value, where everything produced and offered to citizens supports our needs, makes us resonate with the world again, and requires a strict minimum of resources. This is now that we can move from growth addiction to flourishing. It means transitioning from financial to life capital, where people and the planet become our existence's 'raison d'être'.

When economic growth is, life flourishing will be.

When destruction is, regeneration will be.

When frenzy is, slowing down will be.

When productivity is, sufficiency will be.

When busyness is, presence will be.

When private interest is, global commons will be.

When elite is, community will be.

When injustice is, equity will be.

When noise is, silence will be.

When disconnection is, right relationship will be.

To do this, we need to let go of our barriers and welcome the power of imagination, defined by John Dewey[45] as the 'ability to look at things as if they could be otherwise'. Imagination is in decline, with lower levels of creativity in our lives due to the standardisation of our lives. We are too often dazed by society's formatting, forgetting that beyond the virtual structure of our lives lies a need to play and have

---

[45] *John Dewey was an American philosopher, psychologist, and educational reformer whose ideas have been influential in education and social reform.*

fun—coming from our childhood and since then forgotten. In play, there is no right or wrong. The fun aspect of our lives can become a game-changer in moving us forward with a hopeful vision of what is yet to come transcending the boundaries of the existing. Ultimately, life is a big game we are invited to play to pursue a meaningful experience. To have fun in the process of imagination is essential and can happen through three main drivers[46]: playfulness, connection and flow. Playing invites us to let go of the importance given to the outcome to enjoy ourselves in the moment. Connecting guides us by feeling and sensing the relationships around us, facilitating our ability to have fun. Lastly, flowing enables us to be immersed and engaged without giving importance to time but simply living in the moment.

There has not been a more exciting era on Earth to put ourselves in service to the new paradigm. It will take many minds, hearts, and hands to act together, focusing on the power of the collective to unleash the positive impact we can make on the world. Following Rob Hopkins's[47] thinking, 'If we wait for the governments, it'll be too little, too late; if we act as individuals, it'll be too little; but if we act as communities, it might just be enough, just in time'. What if our connection to life, emotions, time, skills, love, passions, and originality could be in service to the future we are dreaming of?

---

[46] *The Power of Fun: How to Feel Alive Again, Catherine Price.*

[47] *From What Is to What If, Rob Hopkins.*

To advance the 'What if?' question, we are called to reinvent the rules of the game we want to play. We are invited to live as part of something bigger than ourselves to win our own game. Something that speaks to who we are collectively on the verge of becoming.

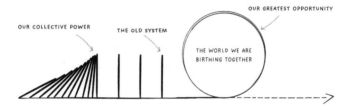

Figure 12: Collectively acting, each and everyone of us can contribute to giving power to the new paradigm. We are given the opportunity to reinvent the rules of a broken system to birth a world that speaks to the life we want to have. This is a call for us to come together and join forces as communities.

KEY TAKEAWAYS

1. There is light in every one of us—a spark that can move mountains. We are intrinsically connected and need to join forces to liberate our creative potential and co-shape a better version of tomorrow.

2. The vested interests of the ones who have built and perpetrated the system will resist until there is a collective awakening. This is our opportunity to create a better version designed by the many for the many.

3. To become agents of change, we need to embrace a whole new form of leadership, moving from 'I' to 'We'. Bio Leadership is our opportunity to reconcile ourselves with the living world while proposing an alternative story that can unleash the power of relationships through compassion, kindness, and reciprocity.

4. There is a new power in the story of inquiring. It is about aligning our heads, hearts, and hands to liberate our global potential. This can make us part of a growing movement of thinkers, creators, and doers.

5. In the cracks of today's society lies the compost for us to plant new seeds. To get rid of the old and welcome the new, we need to liberate our imagination to invent something we have not yet imagined possible.

PRACTICAL REFLECTIONS

→ What seeds would you like to plant in the cracks of the system? How could you nurture them so that they can grow and expand?

→ How can you join existing communities to share your views and learn from others' perspectives?

→ How do you embed the seven principles of Bio Leadership in your life? (resilience, radical collaboration, empowered potential, nurtured connections, harmony, wholeness, and space)

→ How do you leave space for playfulness in your life?

→ How do you let go of the norms, rules and standards to imagine a future that genuinely shuffles the existing to create a radical new way of seeing, living and being?

→ How do you accept not having the answer—inquiring rather than rushing into inadequate solutions?

→ What if tomorrow was your last day on Earth? What would be your most meaningful contribution to leave a positive legacy?

'THE TIME IS NOW.'

As uncertain as the future can seem, the cracks of today's world invite us to reset the rules of the game and work on ourselves to unveil a radically different future. The world, as we know it, is ready to fall apart, calling us to reclaim our inner power and birth a new paradigm driven by the ideals of intergenerational, social and environmental justice.

I often felt overwhelmed by the happenings around the globe, but the light always came back when witnessing the resilience of nature and fellow beings. I especially recall the many times young people and children have given me back hope. Simple eye contact with a stranger or child gazing could bring me back to the duty of acting—with the hope of making change happen so that the next generation thrives.

The sole idea that they will grow up on the planet with the conditions we are creating today often compelled me to contribute right now to what they will experience tomorrow. It helped me grasp the reality of the many generations that could follow us and the world they will inherit. With this in mind, I am no longer a present being but also an ancestor who needs to be accountable to the ones to come. What if the next generations could speak? What if non-humans could speak? What would they call on us to do?

Children's loving energy, playfulness, and ability to return to the basics are a great inspiration for us to be grounded in the simplicity of life. They are early enough to be free of the many limitations explored in the book. They have this fire within themselves that makes them feel as if they could do anything, writing their story on a blank page.

This humanity can be found in each of us. It is where our roots have taken shape. It is where our power lies to write our new story and participate in shaping the future. This is why embracing who you are is essential to contributing to the change you want to see in the world. By knowing yourself better, questioning your perceptions, and letting your imagination guide your aspirations, you are already on the path to making waves of change.

If we had one collective mission in these troubled times, it would be to set up a new dream. This dream calls on us to dare to be curious, creative, and bold to come up with revolutionary thinking. One that adopts a radically new point of view to create disruption—closing the current chapter of humanity fighting against life.

Because today's reality is only a starting point, not a destiny, we are invited to co-design the next chapter of human existence on Earth in symbiosis with life. Beyond the responsibility we are given for generations to come, this is our most significant opportunity to come together for a future more than worth fighting for.

As custodians of life, it is our role to set up this new direction of travel. Our duty is to create a new ideal where we can contribute to support societal flourishing by giving everyone a chance to live in happier, healthier, and safer conditions—in resonance with the living world.

While many of us remain concerned about the change we can make as individuals, there is infinite power in the collective. You are already making an impact with the values you stand for, the actions you take, and the way you show up. With this in mind, you are invited to go beyond what you can accomplish alone.

To change the world, we need conscious people who put their whole selves and talents in service to the future we can collectively dream of—being the artists of our lives. That's the power of our inner worlds. What if you could explore how to put your imagination, passion, and energy as part of the collective?

Be reminded that if you read these words, you have already set yourself on the path to becoming an agent of change. The world needs you as much as you need it to unveil yourself in service to the future.

'Real generosity towards the future lies in giving all to the present.' Inspired by the words of Albert Camus, we are invited to use our collective potential today to become the artisans of tomorrow's future. A future that calls on us to make our lives a meaningful journey, nourishing our heads, hearts, and souls for the better. Together, let's make our collective journey on Earth a wonderful adventure.

Milton Keynes UK
Ingram Content Group UK Ltd.
UKHW041815151124
451262UK00005B/583

9 791041 558216